GREAT PEOPLE MAKE PEOPLE FEEL GREAT

GREAT PEOPLE MAKE PEOPLE FEEL GREAT

How Leaders Elevate Teams with Cloud 9 Thinking

Stuart Holah
Adrian Webster

CAPSTONE
A Wiley Brand

Registered Office(s)
John Wiley & Sons, Inc., 111 River Street, Hoboken, NJ 07030, USA
John Wiley & Sons Ltd, The Atrium, Southern Gate, Chichester, West Sussex, PO19 8SQ, UK

Editorial Office
The Atrium, Southern Gate, Chichester, West Sussex, PO19 8SQ, UK

TNTs™ and Tiny Noticeable Things™ are both Trademarks belonging to Adrian Webster.

For details of our global editorial offices, customer services, and more information about Wiley products visit us at www.wiley.com.

Library of Congress Cataloging-in-Publication Data

ISBN 9780857089533 (Paperback)
ISBN 9780857089595 (ePDF)
ISBN 9780857089588 (ePub)

Cover Design: Wiley
SKY10051206_071423

For Yvonne

Contents

About the Authors

Stuart Holah worked in the asset management industry for 25 years, holding roles including customer services, writing, marketing, business change and leading marketing and business development teams across the UK and Europe. Stuart describes his career as 'showing people they could achieve things they didn't believe they could'.

Adrian Webster is a highly sought after motivational speaker and business coach who is also the author of *Tiny Noticeable Things* and the *Polar Bear Pirates* books, and co-author of *Sort Your Brain Out*. Adrian specialises in inspiring everyday people to deliver exceptional service and helping business leaders to generate extraordinary results.

Despite our inevitable differences in background, experience, temperament and perspective, we have resisted the temptation to write as two separate editorial 'voices,' which we felt would infuriate readers and needlessly complicate what we have tried to present as simple ideas. From this point onwards, the 'voice' of this book is an amalgam of both our experiences, opinions and views. If, in the course of reading this book, you occasionally discern differences in perspective or inconsistencies of viewpoint, then we respectfully apologise for being unable to fully hide the many arguments we enjoyed and which were our inspiration for writing a book together.

Introduction

What Is Cloud Nine?

No-one is exactly sure when 'On Cloud Nine' first entered the English Language. I remember the phrase being in common usage from the 1970s onwards; meaning an extreme state of happiness, bliss or euphoria. Strangely, the exact origin of the expression isn't known and internet searches reveal attributions to meteorological classification systems, which I find unconvincing.

I believe a more likely source could be from the title of a novel written by seventeenth-century Korean aristocrat, politician and scholar Kim Man-Chung (1637–1692). The title translates as 'Dream of the Nine Clouds' and the book explores Buddhist themes; that earthly glory and pleasures don't bring true happiness, reality and dreams are indistinguishable and enlightenment is attained by renouncing commonly desired rewards. In the story, a young monk is banished to experience a life of earthly success, which turns out to be just a dream. When he awakens from his Nine Cloud dream, he realises that lasting fulfilment comes from trying to do what is right, not what is pleasant. The 'Cloud Nine' of Kim Man-Chung's book therefore refers to the attainment of fulfilment through transcendence and enlightenment, quite the opposite of the fleeting state of emotional pleasure that is its modern idiomatic meaning.

I know which I'd choose.

Why Cloud Nine Thinking?

If you want to grow, start by making other people feel taller.

This sentence is one I find myself sharing more than any other when speaking with entrepreneurs, business owners and especially large organisations when they ask how they should attract and retain great talent. These managers know that people are the key to helping them stand head and shoulders above the competition and they are genuine in their desire to foster talent in their teams. Yet most of them are seeking that magic *one thing* they can change. I have to tell them the answer to what they should do differently is '*almost every thing*'.

None of these individual things is particularly hard; in fact you could start doing most of them tomorrow if you wanted to. No single change will bring about the whole transformation that unlocks the collective ability of teams; but shift a few assumptions, challenge some rules and allow people to be their true selves and the talent that is already present in people will show that it is ready to rise. And that's how *Cloud 9 Thinking* was born. Cloud 9 Thinking creates an elevating workplace that lifts people up and helps them feel good about themselves, colleagues and their customers. It's a culture shift that gives people the confidence to bring the undiluted version of themselves into work, inspiring them to get more out of themselves than they thought possible. Once this starts, it's contagious; when people start thinking and working this way it encourages them to want to make others feel a few inches taller too.

Like all change processes, it must come from inside us. People must be willing to give up some comforting and familiar habits and beliefs in order to embrace new viewpoints and practices. Cloud 9 Thinking is about identifying and learning how to relinquish things that we do unthinkingly, and accepting new perspectives relating to how we think about issues, other people and ourselves. It's about simultaneously *letting go* and *embracing*.

As a result, implementing Cloud 9 Thinking takes bold leadership and a willingness to change. It requires leaders who know themselves, who lead by example and take ownership for helping others change. Leaders must dare to do things differently; building a transparent workplace culture where egos are left at the door, diverse thinking is cheered, mistakes are sometimes made and new ideas are celebrated. Their goal is to create a standout workplace and an innovative and winning culture, where no-one is held back from going in pursuit of excellence and everyone shares a simple mantra of: '*Great people, make people feel great.*' By *great people* I don't mean famous, important or high ranking; I simply mean ordinary, everyday people doing an exceptional job as managers, leaders, colleagues or collaborators in whatever business or path of life they have chosen.

This book sets out the nine principles of Cloud 9 Thinking. Though it outlines these principles in a specific sequence, there is no sense of prescription that steps must be taken in any particular order or that each step is relevant to all people or businesses. The Cloud 9 'plan' if there is to be one, must be your own; using as many or as few of these insights as you feel are required to make your people feel taller.

Talent is an anagram of latent. Latent means something already present, waiting to be found. Your challenge is to create the conditions for talent to get released.

I've learned that people will forget what you said, people will forget what you did, but people will never forget how you made them feel.

Maya Angelou

PURSUE MASTERY
TO FIND MEANING, SIMPLIFY
INTEGRITY, STRENGTH AND RESILIENCE
CELEBRATE FAILURE, LEARN FROM SUCCESS
CALMNESS, STRESS AND THE CHOICES WE MAKE
MY MOTIVATION ISN'T YOUR MOTIVATION
EMBRACE THE POWER OF SMALL
SEE PEOPLE AS THEY ARE

LET GO OF PERFECT

Let Go of Perfect

Forget your perfect offering. There is a crack in everything.
That's how the light gets in.

Leonard Cohen

In the Introduction, I shared the spoiler that Cloud 9 Thinking involves relinquishing perceptions that you may previously have held on to quite tenaciously. Many chapters in this book explore common viewpoints that can be challenged and let go. Others introduce new perspectives that might be accepted in their place.

This chapter is most definitely about letting go.

Carrying around inside our minds a perfect idealised conception of how we are meant to act as managers, be viewed by others and even how our projects should turn out, is a tragedy. By tragedy, I don't just mean that it can make you feel unhappy, although it undoubtedly will. I am using tragedy in the original Greek dramatic sense; that a flawed belief or misdirected action will make the downfall of an otherwise capable hero inevitable *even when that bad outcome is the very thing that they are seeking to avoid.*

I am stating very bluntly that if one of your beliefs is that 'perfect' is always the objective, then this view is more likely to undermine your efforts to achieve success than it is to help you get there. Let me share some examples of how this belief can tragically impact the performance of people and teams.

When staff surveys ask people to list the qualities they admire about those in leadership positions, the ability to generate and sustain people's motivation often ranks very highly. Quite right too. But the way in which many managers respond to this leadership requirement is by believing that they need to continually carry around enormous reserves of motivation in order to spread this around every member of their team. As a consequence, when individuals in their teams are not performing as they hope, managers who think this way will consider it to somehow be their own failing and may become disheartened and demotivated. So, if your idea of personal managerial perfection is where your own force of desire will translate magically into individual motivation for every person in your team, then let me set something straight: it won't.

Understanding and accepting that you cannot motivate anyone other than yourself should take a lot of weight off your shoulders. I am a professional motivational speaker and yet I have never motivated anyone except for myself.

What I have done, mainly through storytelling, is clarify objectives and set visions in people's minds; using vivid pictures to hopefully fire imaginations. I have enthused people and hopefully inspired them, but their motivation must come from inside. They must discover their own force of motivation. In **Cloud 4** we will look in more detail at the differences between the emotion of enthusiasm and the psychological drive of motivation, and we will explore how you can inspire and help people find their force of own motivation. For now, I am simply asking you to accept you don't have to single-handedly carry the burden of collective motivation. If that's part of your *perfect*, you can put it down now.

I'd like to try to further unshackle you and your team by challenging another belief that many of us have about 'perfect'. It is often assumed that aiming high and being the best is all about *getting stuff right first time*. In their worthy desire to deliver excellence as an endpoint, many managers believe that everything must be perfect from the start. It often escapes people's minds that unless you happen to be a neurosurgeon, an air traffic controller or a concert pianist, you really don't need to deliver perfection first time, or all of the time.

Most ideas are iterative; you start with an original version that is subsequently refined and improved over time, usually through the input of many different people. In most endeavours, aiming for *right first time* when it applies to ideas is counterproductive. It ignores a lot of other, potentially better, inputs for a start. It is also unattainable and so is not only demotivating and potentially harmful; it's a waste of effort and opportunity. Whenever humans become involved in anything, perfection has a tendency to wander out the door. Beneath the airbrushed surface of any successful business around the world, you would see that they are all made up from an eclectic mix including talented, highly experienced experts as well as a majority of dedicated employees working to achieve common goals. And despite most of these people having given everything their best shot, every one of them will, at some time, have screwed up. Thankfully, they are all imperfect; because if you asked the most highly successful businesses where their very best ideas, innovations and breakthrough discoveries came from, you might be surprised to learn that many of them were the result of a mistake, which was then iterated and improved until the idea became perfect.

In **Cloud 6** we will look at why the process of innovation is actually dependent on failure in order to foster progress. Without errors and mistakes, a lot of new breakthroughs simply wouldn't be discovered; so business leaders must learn to shift the focus of analysing failure, making it less about assessing costs and assigning blame, and more about eliminating poor options and quickly identifying any resulting ideas that can be developed. We must learn from the mindset of researchers in areas like psychology, mathematics, theoretical physics and computing where results of failed experiments and null hypotheses are published in academic papers because of the contribution these failures make to cumulative understanding in these scientific fields.

At the cutting edge of industries like technology services, bioscience and computing, where companies have an entrepreneurial, experimental and academic mindset, it is not uncommon to find a culture of celebrating failure as an opportunity to learn quickly and move forward. Such companies have let go of notions of seeking perfection; they just want to find what works.

There is a far more everyday enemy of success that also stems from notions of perfection, and that is *procrastination*. If we are honest, we may recognise this as much in ourselves as in others. A typical situation might be that a report, presentation or project plan needs writing. The parameters are identified, goals are set and fully understood, and there's no shortage of enthusiasm; and yet nothing is happening. You find yourself over and again staring at an empty screen or blank piece of paper. Why?

There are many reasons this might be. Sometimes it's a prioritisation issue; you or others around you may simply be too busy, distracted or overwhelmed to focus right now on anything relating to the future. This calls for ruthless action. Cloud 5 will look at how to determine which priorities are most important or urgent and offer a framework for deciding whether tasks can be deferred, delegated or even discontinued in order to protect your time for things only you can do. I warn you now that this is not a comfortable exercise. It involves asking whether many day-to-day tasks that you routinely do yourself have become a convenient excuse for not addressing other issues and goals that stretch your capabilities and take you outside your comfort zone. In other words, prioritisation is often not the real reason for procrastination.

If you've already reprioritised other tasks and stared into the abyss of what will happen if you don't get started on a project, and it is *still* not even begun, then I suspect your barrier is a form of perfectionism. A major reason why many people delay starting tasks is because they don't have all the answers. They believe the end result will be better if they wait for *just one more* piece of information. It's an understandable viewpoint because starting without the full facts is an uncomfortable feeling, but this view is also a logical fallacy; part of the process and purpose of any project is to acquire the necessary information as it progresses. Being willing to start something before they have all the information is exactly what distinguishes innovators and entrepreneurs. In their minds, being willing to embark on a course of action when inputs as well as outcomes are still uncertain is not a risky course of action because they trust that answers to questions will emerge. In fact, entrepreneurs are more likely to think that the biggest risk lies in not starting, because that way the answers won't come to them but to their competitors. For tasks involving an element of creativity the challenge is especially difficult because without the flash of inspiration from your creative muse it can be difficult to know how to start. As we examine in **Cloud 9**, creativity relies on input from your subconscious mind and the very act of starting a project can trigger the familiar routines and thought processes that free and unblock your subconscious. If you find yourself in this situation, remember what poet and author Charles Ghigna says so eloquently; *'Don't search for inspiration . . . just start your work and you will see that it will soon find you.'*

For most of us, the best way to counter perfection-based procrastination is to focus on a process, not an outcome. For example, when I set out to write a 200-page book, I didn't wait until I felt I could write all 200 pages perfectly. Instead, I broke the task down. Starting with just the barest outline, I next filled in the missing information by asking the businesses and people I work with what their biggest workplace issues were and what questions their teams were asking. I then had a series of chapter topics and could start authoring a page or a sentence at a time, testing my ideas on anyone who would listen, expanding these ideas and making amendments and corrections as I went. I didn't worry that my early ideas and drafts were frankly pretty poor. I focused on finding a writing process that worked for me, and once I'd started I found that the task could only move forwards.

As a writer, I'm swimming in a small pond compared with Pulitzer Prize-winning author Jane Smiley. Jane has over 30 books to her credit and must be more than familiar with the tyranny of a blank page and the intimidation of deadlines. That's probably why her words on this subject are so insightful: '*Every first draft is perfect, because all a first draft has to do is exist.*'

Procrastination is normal and we all do it to a degree. Excessive procrastination can be based on notions of perfectionism and is a common block to success. You may be interested to learn that there is a name for an obsessive fear of imperfection: *atelophobia*. I am not suggesting that people who procrastinate are suffering from atelophobia. However, I do believe that perfectionists are unnecessarily hard not only on themselves, but on those around them.

If workplace goals are not met because projects don't get initiated on time and you suspect perfectionism lies at the heart of this, then the problem runs deeper than a lack of immediate productivity. Procrastination is a workplace disease that has a high impact on the overall well-being of your team. Individuals who procrastinate excessively can suffer from anxiety and low self-esteem; the more prolonged any delay, the more anxious they become. They are not only more prone to workplace stress as individuals but they can be difficult and uncomfortable colleagues; not getting the best out of teammates.

As a leader, you can help your team overcome perfection-based procrastination by openly challenging a viewpoint that perfection is always the goal, especially at the outset of a project. You can also reassure people that they can learn to live with the discomfort of not knowing all the answers they will need. But by far the greatest difference will come when you back all this up by consciously fostering a culture where it is OK for people to admit that they don't know all the answers, when it is permitted to make mistakes and where people are encouraged to ask for help whenever it is needed. How to do this is in fact the topic of **Cloud 7**, which looks at building team resilience.

The last point I want to make in this opening chapter is one I personally consider to be amongst the most important in this book. For what seems to be an increasing number of people in the workplace, a desire to live up to some perfect and unrealistic conception of *how they should be* is so overwhelming that they constantly think they are failing and falling short. They suffer from a nagging insecurity that they *don't deserve to be here* in their role. Instead of seeing perfection for the myth that it is and just trying to do the best they can in their jobs, such people suffer a crippling anxiety and become more determined than ever to avoid making mistakes. It is not difficult to see how this can have catastrophic and self-fulfilling consequences: if people are scared to make mistakes, they are resistant to trying anything new and therefore deny themselves opportunities to learn to overcome their fears.

Today, the term *imposter syndrome* is widely used to describe such feelings of self-doubt and inadequacy in the workplace. Before the 1980s, imposter syndrome wasn't a term used outside the sphere of academic psychology. Today it is a leading topic and studies have stated that around 70 per cent of people will experience at least one such lifetime episode of feeling this way.[1]

What I would like to explore here is an idea that for most of us, some feelings of work-related self-doubt and anxiety are an entirely normal reaction to particular situations and are also strongly linked to our mental template of what constitutes perfection. I'd also like to make it very clear that, in trying to take a slightly wider perspective on this issue, I am not in any way seeking to diminish the genuine suffering that those with imposter syndrome undergo. Thankfully, this is now a clinically recognised psychological condition and there are a range of therapies and services available to help people.

A characteristic of someone with severe imposter syndrome is that they would experience their negative feelings as overwhelming, debilitating and permanent because they arise from deep-rooted beliefs and insecurities about themselves. For the rest of us, feelings of self-doubt may be an entirely rational human reaction to unfamiliar situations. Self-doubt may also be a measure of the degree to which we can learn to manage our own conception of 'perfect' as it relates to different aspects of our workplace performance. I would go so far as to say that some occasional feelings of doubt are positive. They are reassuring proof that you have enough insight to anticipate that an environment or a challenge you face will require you to develop skills and abilities you may not feel confident about. Recognising and acknowledging where you need to develop is a great strength. If you don't believe me, think about anyone you have ever met who is blissfully unaware of their own shortcomings, limitations and ignorance. They are a person who lacks insight and there are more of them out there than you would believe.

As we shall explore further in **Cloud 5**, human brains evolved to deal with the world as it existed 300,000 years ago. Despite all the changes in the way we live now, the fundamental neural wiring of our brains hasn't changed a great deal since then. Consequently, our own brains can create perceptions, emotions and biases that are not only poorly adapted to today's modern world; we are often completely unaware that this is happening. One such example is the so-called *negativity bias*, which describes the psychological basis for why we find bad news easier to believe than good news and tend to dwell on our own and other people's negative perceptions rather than positive viewpoints.

The explanation for why our brain works this way goes back a long way.

When our ancestors lived in caves and ran away from sabre-toothed tigers, there was a significant evolutionary advantage in having a brain that could focus very close attention on aspects of our surroundings which could be threatening or harmful to us. The brain developed a mechanism designed to give priority to bad news and recognise it faster next time. The better this mechanism worked, the more evolutionary advantage it conferred and the more the genes responsible for this ability were passed down to all the descendants who hadn't been eaten by predators. Eventually, this brain mechanism evolved to work really well indeed.

The part of the brain that processes our response to events and experiences is the *amygdala*, which is a complex structure of cells in the midbrain making up part of our limbic system. Neuroanatomists have shown that around two-thirds of the neurons in the amygdala are pre-wired to recognise bad news rather than positive stimuli, and will preferentially transfer negative events and experiences much more quickly to our memory. In comparison, positive events and experiences usually need to be held in conscious awareness for a period of

10 seconds or more before they will form enduring memories. Our brain's bias towards perceiving and storing negative news doesn't stop there. Not only are negative event and experience memories stored more readily and more quickly, research shows that they are retained for longer than positive memories in what psychology researchers have termed positive–negative asymmetry. We are quite literally wired to over prioritise bad news.

Now we can begin to understand why we are more likely to dwell on negative workplace comments or instances where we didn't perform as we hoped, whilst under-estimating compliments and positive performances. Even when the positives significantly outweigh negatives, our brain's in-built negativity bias can create a different perception. Of course, the human brain is more complicated than a simple memory-creating system, so we do possess the intellectual means to over-ride our evolutionary default setting. Many factors including our upbringing, our social relationships and other inputs determine how we interpret the information we hold inside our memories, and the single most important factor we can control is how we create a mindful dialogue around the good and positive aspects of our lives. As explained earlier, positive events and experiences will form stronger and more enduring memories when they are held in conscious awareness; when you pause and allow yourself time to actively think about them.

If this bias towards overweighting negative experiences is part of the explanation for *how* imposter syndrome can occur, it can't be the explanation for *why* there has been such a recent explosion in the number of people reporting that they feel phony and underconfident in their workplace or in other situations. After all, human brains have been wired the same way for 300,000 years. What else has changed? I'd like to suggest that the change in how people feel about themselves is linked to changes in more recent decades, particularly around our consumption of social media. We have fostered a society where we continually and often unconsciously compare ourselves, our achievements, abilities and indeed our whole lives with other people. We are as helpless to turn off this unhealthy aspect of our thinking as we are powerless to turn off our smartphones. Even more worrying, we cannot even recognise the subtle ways in which these comparisons are influencing our thinking. For example, if you are videoconferencing with colleagues who are working from home, it is almost guaranteed that people will have behind them an artfully curated background containing a tidy bookshelf, tasteful lamp, family photo, holiday souvenir, degree or diploma certificate and some sports or professional award. It's an arms race. Choose to compete if you like with your own carefully arranged backdrop, but don't beat yourself up if your whole home doesn't look like the immaculately presented scene behind someone's head on your screen. Because neither does theirs – it's all just appearances.

In the modern workplace, there seems to be a culture of downplaying the effort we put into our accomplishments. When did it become uncool to admit you worked hard? When I started in business, I wanted to be seen as hard working. Nowadays, we may spend all night writing a report only to tell our colleagues and bosses 'Oh, it's just something I put together quickly.' Again, see this for what it is; part of the arms race, not something objective you should compare your report-writing ability with.

Comparison-based self-beliefs can be especially damaging when they become self-fulfilling. Presenting to meetings and handling formal social situations are both learned skills. These skills may come more easily to those with an outgoing disposition, but we can all become better. If no-one let you in on the secret that the most accomplished presenters have, despite what they may say, probably rehearsed endlessly, you might think that you could never become a confident presenter. And if you believe you won't, then you won't.

How are we meant to be confident in our abilities when other people are creating an illusion about theirs? Because even when we do something well, that positive experience may not change our self-belief if we put our own success down to hard work, but attribute other people's success to ability? We must learn to see this differently. I like to imagine that my work life is a bit like playing a game of poker. Each card in my hand represents an experience, skill or ability that I bring to the table. Like cards, these skills can be changed and upgraded when I am given an opportunity, and I take calculated risks based on what I absolutely know for certain I have in my hand. But what if the other players at the table were playing a subtly different game, in which they were not just occasionally bluffing, but were allowed to tell outright lies about what cards they held and what hands they played. How might you play the game differently, without accusing your co-workers of being frauds and phonies and demanding that they show their hand at every turn? One answer is that you could start to lie too. Or you could accept that you can't see what hand other people hold, and you can't necessarily take people at face value. All you can focus on is playing your hand as best you can and stop beating your-self up with unhelpful comparisons. You can also help other people understand these issues too. As a business leader, you can foster an environment where it is accepted that feelings of self-doubt are a normal human reaction to unfamiliar situations. You can recognise that such anxieties are common around transitions to new roles or responsibilities and par-ticularly amongst younger or newer team members – and ensure these people are supported.

But the issue is, sadly, really much bigger than just a workplace issue. I'd like to end this chapter with a quote from Stephen R. Covey.

If we are not secure in our self-definition, we look to the social mirror for our identity and approval. Our concept of ourselves comes from what others think of us. We find ourselves gearing our lives to meet their expectations. The more we live what others expect of us, the more insecure and pretentious we become.

[...]

If the vision we have of ourselves comes from the social mirror – from the opinions, perceptions and paradigms of the people around us – our view of ourselves is like a reflec-tion in the crazy mirror at the carnival.

These words sound like a warning of the perils of mod-ern social media; about the empty vanity of creating a man-ufactured online version of ourselves and measuring our worth through others' validation of this, whilst knowing that even we don't live up to this idealised image of ourselves.

Yet Stephen Covey wrote his words in 1992; years before ubiquitous internet usage and a decade or more before the social media explosion.

We can't put the social media genie back in the bottle, or re-wire the human brain so it isn't continually making negatively biased comparisons with other people's lives and achievements. In **Cloud 7** we will look at what you can do as a business leader to play your part in creating a workplace environment that is free of distortions. What would happen if everyone in your team grasped that it's their choice whether or not they constantly want to be perfect in the world generated by the media and people posting illusions on social media; but they knew that in your business, *you'd just like them to be themselves*? It's guaranteed there will be an instant, possibly audible, release. With this weight off their shoulders, everyone will suddenly look and feel taller and they will be set free to concentrate all their efforts on doing a great job.

PURSUE MASTERY
TO FIND MEANING, SIMPLIFY
INTEGRITY, STRENGTH AND RESILIENCE
CELEBRATE FAILURE, LEARN FROM SUCCESS
CALMNESS, STRESS AND THE CHOICES WE MAKE
MY MOTIVATION ISN'T YOUR MOTIVATION
EMBRACE THE POWER OF SMALL

SEE PEOPLE AS THEY ARE
LET GO OF PERFECT

Cloud
2

See People as They Are

We don't see things as they are. We see them as we are.

Anaïs Nin

The next time you find yourself sitting on a train pulling into a crowded station, take a moment to peer out of the window at all the people standing on the packed platform. Observe the infinite number of variations in their features and notice that not one face is identical to another.

The same is true for personalities. Out of 8 billion people on the planet, no-one has the exact same mix of personality traits as you, me – or anyone else. For as long as humankind has committed ideas to record, it has sought to explain the variation in our temperaments and describe the distinctive characteristics or qualities observed in different individuals.

Today, we can laugh at how earlier thinkers believed this worked. *Hippocrates* (400 BCE) and *Galen* (140 CE) thought that different personality dispositions were conferred by variations in bodily fluids or *humours*. Remarkably, this viewpoint survived for over 2,000 years until the end of the nineteenth century; there's a passing lesson here that the longevity and apparent permanence of ideas doesn't necessarily mean that those ideas are true.

Only when new explanations emerged from the twentieth-century sciences of neurobiology and psychology did we begin to understand the complex mechanisms behind variation in people's personalities. Modern theories explain that personality develops in a way which is partly determined by inherited genetics and partly in response to family, social and other experiences particularly in youth. Arguing about the relative contributions of these complex factors keeps thousands of psychologists employed. Perhaps in another 2,000 years they'll have an even better idea.

For now, the main purpose of this chapter is to look at *how you can build stronger teams and foster better collaboration by understanding how different personalities interact*. It's a very worthwhile goal because it means you can achieve more by using what you already have – the people in your team.

To illustrate an important point about all classification systems, it's worth looking at the fundamental personality types set out by the Greek physician Hippocrates. Whilst the mechanism behind Hippocrates' classifications is not accepted today and his categories are superseded by more complex models based on measurement of individual trait characteristics, I am sure you can identify people you know in his characterisation of four temperaments.

Sanguine – a sanguine personality type is outgoing, positive and confident. They are sociable, upbeat and quickly establish rapport and friendships.

Phlegmatic – this personality is relaxed, calm, sympathetic and trusting. Phlegmatic individuals enjoy harmony, know themselves well and value loyalty.

Choleric – choleric personalities are ambitious, confident and determined. These highly active and driven characters are also restless and often impatient.

Melancholic – melancholic characters are quiet types who keep to themselves. They are serious, logical thinkers who tend to be both meticulous and cautious.

Did you recognise other people or even yourself in any of these four category descriptions? Did you find that no-one fitted exactly in one category but tended to possess qualities listed in two or more of these temperament types? That's because any classification system that tries to squeeze the entire infinite variety of human personality into fewer than 8 billion buckets is bound to fail. When classifying anything, compromises have to be made. A system with a large number of categories may lead to fewer exceptions, but it won't provide much clarity. A system with fewer categories may provide a much clearer model or explanation but will work less well as a definitive sorting mechanism. When using any classification system to deal with natural rather than man-made phenomena, we must remember that all possible systems will be flawed; there will have been a trade-off between usefulness and completeness. That's not the same as saying such systems aren't useful; they help us make sense of an otherwise unmanageable volume of information and in doing so help us simplify and refine our ideas. As we shall explore in **Cloud 8** some of the world's cleverest thinkers have been big fans of simple. And we should be too.

A key message of this chapter is that we will heed all the warnings about the limitations of classification systems. We will acknowledge that people come from diverse backgrounds and starting points. We will recognise that people are at different stages of their working life; one workplace could encompass four or five different generations, all thinking and working differently and shaped by different experiences. Yet despite knowing all this, we will go ahead anyway and try to represent this variety in a classification system. Our only excuse will be that that the system we've chosen is enormously valuable in understanding why people are good at what they do, and can help managers identify and coach people's strengths, mitigate weaknesses and build effective, harmonious and high-achieving teams.

The basis on which we are going to outline differences between people is often referred to as *working style*. Your *working style* is the way you go about the day-to-day tasks of your job. It describes the particular ways in which you approach tasks, solve problems and communicate and interact with other people. Some people analyse, others imagine. Some people plan, others create. Some of us work better collaboratively and others produce their best efforts when left alone. We are all different; everyone has their own working style, which reflects their unique psychological make-up. Although broadly related to personality types, working styles are not the same thing. As we enter the workplace each day we change; we adapt our behaviours, we adjust our outward persona in order to meet the different expectations on us. Working styles are different to personality characteristics because they are specific to the demands and tasks of the workplace and the pressures and responsibilities of our jobs.

Just as with descriptions of personality, classification of working styles inevitably involves simplification and approximation. Depending on which expert you believe, there are between 4 to 16 different profiles describing our in-work behaviour. You could choose any working style classification system out of the literally dozens that exist and you and your team would undoubtedly benefit. However, over the years I have adopted a system which uses six broad categories, which I find accommodates most of us. You may be familiar with systems that use other labels; my own preferred system uses *Driver, Analyst, Creator, Orchestrator, Delegator* and *Sociable*.

Driver

Upside – Drivers take decisive action. They are organised and task-focused individuals who create their own process to work quickly and efficiently. Drivers challenge the team to improve and push on when others may quit.

Flipside – Drivers may forget to consult and communicate widely, yet vent their frustration at colleagues who are not on the same page. Drivers can't abide inaction and need to feel in control.

Analyst

Upside – Analysts are diligent, logical and data-oriented; making them careful decision makers and good problem solvers. They uphold project aims and ensure deadlines and budgets are met.

Flipside – Analysts don't seek involvement and may not interact with the wider team. They require a stable work environment, with clear organisational processes and structure, to perform at their best.

Creator

Upside – Creators are big-picture thinkers; generating ideas, finding solutions and creating vision. They are comfortable innovating, taking risks and ignoring tradition. Creators act as catalysts for change and stop businesses stagnating.

Flipside – Creators make decisions based on intuitive hunches not analysis. They can procrastinate and don't enjoy follow-through.

Orchestrator

Upside – Orchestrators hear your business pulse and the outside world heartbeat. By networking and harnessing resources, orchestrators make things possible. When Creators originate ideas, Orchestrators happily pull them forward without any author's pride.

Flipside – Orchestrators experience their rush of enthusiasm at the birth of a new project and can lose momentum and fail to follow things up in the final project stages.

Delegator

Upside – Delegators have a talent for stepping back to see the full scale of an issue. As detached logical observers who recognise others' abilities, they excel at delegating, planning and helping others focus on their tasks.

Flipside – The more that Delegators delegate, the fewer tasks they retain beyond more delegating! If they don't pitch in to help colleagues, they can be perceived as not pulling their weight, workshy or even manipulative.

Sociable

Upside – Sociables are the glue holding teams together. They are supportive, expressive, and emotionally oriented and excel in building relationships with colleagues. Because they are good listeners and diplomats they avoid interpersonal conflict and create team cohesion, inclusion, communication and interaction.

Flipside – Sociables do not work quickly, and their caution and unwillingness to take sides may mean they put off decisive action. Sociables don't like pressure or uncertainty, and their low-key profile can leave them feeling unnoticed, unappreciated and demotivated.

I hope you found yourself in there somewhere. The first point to note is that there is no *best* working style. These classifications are qualitative, not quantitative; there are no scores or ratings. As we shall see, each of these types is vitally important to the functioning of an effective team. Don't worry if you straddle categories and demonstrate characteristics of more than one. As we already highlighted, classifications systems are always an approximation for the real-world diversity of people; if something or someone doesn't fit, that doesn't mean the ideas behind the classification aren't useful.

The second point to note is that strengths and weaknesses come in combination and you can't have one without the other. Each working style not only reflects abilities and strengths, but also blind-spots. I still remember the first time I was told that each of my strengths had its corresponding weakness; like two sides of a coin. It felt as if someone had turned on a light. I suddenly understood why I found some things easy and other tasks impossibly hard or off-putting. And as I thought about it afterwards, I realised that even highly successful people like sports stars can exhibit a notable strength that is offset by a weakness; a tennis player with a powerful backhand but a weak forehand, or a golfer with an exceptional long game who is inconsistent on the greens. Our strengths are the flipside of our weaknesses. Much later, I came to understand that in order to fully benefit from our strengths we must also recognise, understand and adapt for where we are less capable.

For example; when someone is very driven, it's likely they lead from the front and move quickly to exploit any opportunities they spot. I've no doubt this approach works and I've seen many outstanding teams run this way. But colleagues of a person like this can feel as if they trail in their wake; if communication is lacking, other people feel disenfranchised from all that success. That's the flipside. Conversely, colleagues of a very collaborative, communicative and consensual leader will fully understand business priorities and the part they can each play. However, it may be less likely that this leader can rapidly take advantage of business opportunities. Again, there's a flipside.

Partly, the answer for the driven leader is to understand their deficiency and prioritise communication and consensus. Similarly, the collaborative leader could ensure they respond more rapidly to important marketplace changes. But the most powerful benefit of thinking in terms of working styles is that it brings the option to look at colleagues and ask *'who has the particular strength to help me in an area where I am not so strong?'* This is, after all, the point of teamwork.

A group of individuals doing the same thing in the same way is not a team. It's only a group. A real team is a combination of people who blend their work styles, to operate in a subtly different way; sharing tasks according to strengths in order to achieve a common goal.

Within teams, people tend to naturally gravitate towards roles that play to their strengths, but they may give less thought to whether their weaknesses will hold them back. Sometimes, developing an awareness of weaknesses is all that is required; we can practice and develop our competence or put in extra effort to compensate for what we find harder. If you are choosing candidates for a role or putting new teams together, ensuring that you have all the necessary workplace styles and strengths represented within a team is invaluable. Also helpful is balancing skills of key staff who may benefit from working in closer partnership with specific individuals whose skillset brings a strength that will offset a particular weakness.

If you can't see much work-style variation between the people around you, then I'd suggest your team or organisation has a problem. Maybe not immediately, but possibly in the future when you are pulled in so many directions that your own flipside becomes more exposed. If your team included people whose work style was very different, it might be easier to find someone whose strengths exactly matched areas in which you needed support. If you sat down right now and tried to picture a person with a complete opposite skillset to yourself, you may just have written the profile for the best hire you could possibly ever make.

Having said earlier that there is no *best* working style and that each skillset is invaluable in contributing to overall business success, you'd expect the credit and recognition to be spread evenly. The reality is very different. The lion's share of credit often falls to Drivers, Creators and Analysts. That's partly because projects would quickly stall if they didn't contribute their part of a process on time. But it's also because it's easy to see what they do; you don't have to be a close colleague to understand their contribution. It can be seen from a distance including by those higher up in the corporate hierarchy. Delegators also tend to get noticed because they are usually in charge.

By contrast, Orchestrators and Socials are typically the underrated and under-valued skillsets within an organisation. Note that I said *organisation* and not team. Immediate team members of Orchestrators and Socials will be in no doubt over the value these people bring; by networking and harnessing resources in the case of Orchestrators, or creating harmony and cementing relationships in the case of Socials. But their low-key profile doesn't help their visibility within a bigger organisation.

I once worked with a colleague I shall call Will. He was modest, perceptive and diplomatic and knew everyone at their level in every department. Customers and suppliers adored Will, as did teammates because he was the glue that that bound us all together. No birthday went unnoticed. No opportunity to share our team's successes with a contributing department was wasted. When anyone had a problem, Will was the listener. In terms of working style preferences, Will was a Social/ Orchestrator. Any company would be lucky to have him. But come the annual pay round, I would dread seeing my very driven boss to discuss Will. My boss didn't understand what Will brought to the team as his individual campaign results were not amongst the best. One year, when the issue of Will's results arose, I asked my boss to set numbers aside and tell me whether he believed Will helped the team become more effective. He conceded that he did, but that it couldn't be quantified. I agreed it was hard to set an exact figure on it, but asked whether he thought the contribution was closer to 50 per cent or 10 per cent. He saw exactly where I was going and chose 10 per cent. I then explained that if Will helped 10 people perform at 110 per cent capacity, then even with no results of their own, his contribution was 100 per cent. Since we were a team of 12, he was underpaying him. It was the first time I had seen my boss speechless. He agreed Will's raise. In subsequent years, my boss always made a point of asking how Will was getting along.

The moral of the story is that it can be easy to underestimate Orchestrators and Socials. If you have someone in your team who boosts morale, draws the team together and ensures good relations with customers, suppliers and other departments; then please recognise and reward them. They are someone whose skill is drawing more out of others than they can directly produce themselves by making everything work in harmony.

I liken these often under-valued people to an egg. Imagine you want to make an omelette and you open the fridge. You have pancetta, mushrooms, cheese, peppers, spinach, fresh coriander leaves – but no eggs. All those impressive ingredients are no good on their own because they lack the one humble ingredient that will bind them together perfectly. Some people are eggs. Cherish them.

My closing point in this chapter is a warning about taking the perspective offered by *work-style preferences* too far.

Work styles are a valuable tool to help understand people's specific workplace abilities and how these predispose them to excel in particular areas, complement colleagues and, as a result, contribute to more effective and productive teams. But we must never forget that each person is far more than the cumulative sum of their workplace talents. What I mean is that people have so many other positive attributes that they can bring with them into work when they are given permission. People can bring things to the table that go way beyond their job specification. These are often immeasurable qualities that may not be that apparent at first glance. These abilities may be hidden away and in some cases people may be completely oblivious that they have them. Consider the quality of humility; can someone truly possess the quality of humility and also be aware that they have this?

OK, that's a humorous example just to illustrate that people can't always know how powerful their unique and human qualities are. I call these *pocket powers*: human qualities that someone can share with others when required. For example, you may notice that whenever someone in your team has a personal problem, they seek out a particular individual. It is highly likely that this individual's pocket power is empathy, or sympathy or maybe even relationship counselling. Another person in your team may always be making people laugh and defusing otherwise tense or stressful situations. It might be that someone else is a constant source of support for people who may be struggling in their role. Some people bring clarity of understanding. And one of the most valuable if you have one in your team is the person who is the reassuring and steady influence when the sticky stuff hits the fan, maybe even standing up to take some splatter to the face in order to protect others.

If you are fortunate enough to have neurodiverse people in your team, you will already be aware of the unique abilities and perspectives they can bring; as well as differences in social preferences, communication and the way they view the world. Neurodivergence affects people in different ways, so no two individuals are alike; but differences in viewpoint may be expressed through heightened curiosity, imagination, innovation and focus. Leading organisations who value problem solving and originality actively hire neurodiverse talent.

Despite *pocket powers* being immensely powerful qualities that unite teams and help create close-knit family-like environments, they tend not to even appear on the radar of many organisations. The reason is as obvious as it is sad: since these qualities are not always easy to spot and are regarded by a lot of managers as being difficult to measure, they go unrecognised and unrewarded. They don't fit into any tick-box system.

I suspect there is also the factor that not all pocket powers are going to be well liked by management or other team members. Just like our work style preferences, pocket powers have both a positive aspect, and a flipside. Somebody who possesses clarity of thought might also express opinions that are, on occasion, a little more direct than people want to hear at that moment. The office joker may bring valuable release during times of tension, but they may also bring too much levity at other times. Not all pocket powers are compatible with a smooth ride towards achieving your team's objectives. However, it's worth holding in your mind that whilst 'smooth' might be easiest to manage and therefore preferred by most managers, sometimes 'extreme' is needed to get the job done. Pocket powers can make all the difference in those make-or-break situations where other teams would stumble.

One particular pocket power that illustrates this is when you have someone in your team who has a naturally contrarian mindset. This is not the same as an oppositional mindset when somebody deliberately sets out to disagree with or antagonise other people. A contrarian naturally sees the world differently to others; they see opportunity where others don't but they can also perceive risks and failings that other people can't see. As a result, they can be written off as simply oppositional and labelled as antagonistic or disruptive because they question the status quo. Such a person may never win the 'most popular team member' award, but they may in fact be the most valuable player on your entire team.

By seeing things that others don't and '*speaking truth to power*' contrarians can provide an essential conduit to senior management, even though what they say may go against the flow and isn't what people want to hear. As a by-product of their pocket power, contrarians can create agitation. Agitators stir up discussion, they force people to look at things differently and find alternative ways to do things. They can be a powerful force for change by providing 'grit' within a team. Grit will cause friction in any well-oiled machine, but bear in mind that this same irritant also causes pearls to form when a piece of sand lodges inside an oyster. No grit, no friction. No grit, no pearls.

Remember, your job as a manager is not to create the team that is most easy to manage, even though that is often what your seniors would like you to do. Instead, you must champion the extremities of talent in your team if that is what is required to take performance to the next level and achieve excellence. This will require a 3D perspective, looking beyond merely *managing* people but *seeing* each person as they really are; not just as job titles or as talents or as work-style labels but as three-dimensional, completely unique individuals with so much more to offer than what first meets the eye. This will, of course, mean proactively going out of your way to really get to know them, to put your head inside their world for a while and find out what really makes them tick. By doing so, you not only show them how much you appreciate them as a person as well as for what they contribute, you may also help them discover – or gain confidence to uncover – what they have hidden in that pocket of theirs.

When I think back to the most inspiring leader I ever worked with, what I remember beyond his analytical sharpness, his humility and his ability to inspire with visions that were as crystal clear as they were ambitious, was his acceptance of people for whoever they were. His simple, natural curiosity about people meant he connected with employees at every level of the organisation without regard to their seniority. He didn't see roles, he just saw people; and he gave them the freedom to bring their whole, complete self into work, pocket powers and all. He saw value in grit, welcomed grit when he came across it and even thanked the people who gave it to him.

Hello Robert. I'm sorry I never fully thanked you.

PURSUE MASTERY
TO FIND MEANING, SIMPLIFY
INTEGRITY, STRENGTH AND RESILIENCE
CELEBRATE FAILURE, LEARN FROM SUCCESS
CALMNESS, STRESS AND THE CHOICES WE MAKE
MY MOTIVATION ISN'T YOUR MOTIVATION

EMBRACE THE POWER OF SMALL
SEE PEOPLE AS THEY ARE
LET GO OF PERFECT

Cloud
3

Embrace the Power of Small

There are these two young fish swimming along and they happen to meet an older fish swimming the other way, who nods at them and says 'Morning boys. How's the water?'

And the two young fish swim on for a bit, and then eventually one of them looks over at the other and goes 'What the hell is water?'

David Foster Wallace

Yes, it's a silly story, a profound story or a profoundly silly story – depending on your viewpoint. It is also a particular favourite of mine, because it can illustrate that oftentimes people really don't give much thought to big things all around them. The more ubiquitous those things are, the less we actually take notice.

If you're still not convinced, imagine the following situation. You've walked into a car showroom; it's a vast temple of plate glass and architectural steel. You can literally see your reflection in the polished tile floor, and rows of spotless cars

are artfully lit by carefully arranged lighting. A car manufacturer or distributor has invested millions to make it look
like that. Are you more likely to buy a car in that dealership
because of these surroundings? No – because they all look
like that. It's exactly what you'd expect; it's all big stuff that
we've got used to. It's just water.

If you're anything like me, or frankly anybody else I've
ever discussed car purchases with, you're much more likely
to be influenced by whether the receptionist looks up and
smiles as you enter, if he or she takes your name and asks
if you'd like coffee or tea. By whether a salesperson appears
promptly with the same drink you asked for, greets you by
name, introduces themself and lets you take all the time you
need to find out what you want to know.

I would wager that if every one of those simple things has
ever happened faultlessly and in that order, then you were
either very lucky or buying a *very* expensive car. Because this
is not the experience of most ordinary customers. Despite
these being such basic actions, they don't appear to be the
norm. Why? None of these aspects of customer service are
particularly difficult; they are easy, they could be taught to
staff in under a day. They don't cost millions to implement
like building a shiny great showroom; they cost nothing and
they are the very things that are most likely to determine
whether we choose to pursue our purchase with that dealership, or take our custom elsewhere.

The point of this example is not to finger-point and single out car dealerships; I could have chosen examples from
anything from hotel receptions to furniture superstores, air-
line check-ins to banks. The common factor is that these and
other businesses spend a fortune trying to get the big stuff

right, only to serve up a mediocre or worse experience when it comes to actually engaging with customers every day. They have the advertising budgets, the brand image, the impressive premises and the fancy décor; then they put staff in customer-facing roles that either don't want to make a connection or don't know how to.

To borrow a sporting expression, these companies are 'all swing but no ding'; they have made all the expensive and eye-catching corporate effort, but at the point of customer engagement, which really matters, there is no meaningful impact. These companies look the part and appear to be busy going through the motions of serving me, but I'm not getting any sense that they understand or care. There's no hitting my sweet spot, let alone knocking me out of the park. Despite all the corporate bling, I'm just not feeling any ding.

And yet it could be so different. By focusing on getting small customer-facing things right, these businesses could connect better, create an outstanding customer experience and truly differentiate themselves. I call these small things TNTs – or *Tiny Noticeable Things*. I'm a bit obsessional about TNTs; so much so that I wrote a whole book on the subject. TNTs are all the little things that people don't need to do, but when we *do* do them, they can have a seismic impact and make a huge difference. They could be as small as a smile, a 'thank you' or remembering someone's name. These actions may be tiny, but they are highly effective and create the biggest and longest-lasting images in people's minds. They show that your company cares, and they make the difference between a mediocre customer experience and an outstanding one. Most of these TNTs cost little or nothing to implement. Without a requirement for a huge budget to get started, TNTs are disruptive; they level the playing field between large and small companies. They are everyday secret weapons that allow the smallest businesses to outshine even giant competitors.

If you doubt the colossal transformative value of multiple small, incremental actions then let us return to our sporting analogy of swings and dings. In cricket, baseball, tennis and golf and no doubt many other pursuits, elite players devote the entirety of their sporting careers to a relentless quest to adapt or perfect their swing, stroke or serve. Their ability to consistently hit the sweet spot doesn't happen by chance. Perfecting their technique takes years of dedicated practice and relentless determination as well as unwavering support from coaches and other people around them. Each coaching session is likely to focus on not on making big changes, but on small adaptations. Overall performance is dissected into a sequence of tiny actions, which can be refined, repeated and rehearsed until they are completely automatic; they reach a point at which they are so instinctive that they cannot be unlearned. This is what differentiates the true sporting greats; they hit the sweet spot all the time, they make every swing a ding regardless of the opponent, the circumstances or the pressure because they do it without conscious thought. They do it because they've literally forgotten what it was like to do it any other way. And they've reached that point through addressing a whole multitude of *little* things. Little things truly matter.

Imagine what would happen in your business if your customer-facing employees saw every interaction as an opportunity to *simply get the little things consistently right by focusing on delivering TNTs?* Your customers would be blown away; any expectation they had formed based on their dealings with other organisations would be completely surpassed.

I'd now like to let you into the secret of *why* TNTs work; how it is that such small things have a disproportionately positive impact on our perception of service. It is because of a peculiar feature of our brain's response to positive experiences. When we attain an object or a goal we perceive as rewarding – which may be as simple as getting a smile or interacting pleasantly with someone – part of our brain's limbic system called the tegmentum releases a burst of *dopamine*. This neurotransmitter chemical not only creates our immediate sensation of pleasure; it switches on neural processes that embed pleasurable memories. This motivation–reward mechanism ensures that we learn to repeat rewarding experiences and is the basis for our deep-seated survival drives to eat, drink, reproduce and perform activities to gain resources.

The original biological purpose of pleasure is to ensure survival; this explains why we experience modest pleasure from a minor reward like a small meal, and much more intense pleasure from encountering an opportunity to reproduce or provide parental nurturing, which have a greater survival value. However, the scale of the dopamine response does not appear to vary as widely as we might expect between trivial and very significant positive events; the response seems to depend far more on the difference between our *expectation* and our *experience* of events.

It means all positive experiences are perceived as rewarding, no matter whether they are small or big. And it means we perceive greater reward when our expectations are exceeded.

So small, but unanticipated, positive experiences can affect us more than larger, expected, positive experiences!

That is peculiar, and you've probably realised that '*small unanticipated positive experiences*' is a pretty good working definition for TNTs. When we do many little positive things for customers, particularly when they are not expected, we are sending their dopamine levels soaring; that's how TNTs work. No-one can turn off this mechanism. Whilst some people are more overt in how they experience or display pleasurable emotion, we all share one brain blue-print. Not every customer will smile in response to TNTs, but that doesn't mean TNTs aren't working.

Interestingly, a small amount of dopamine is released in our brains merely in *anticipation* of a rewarding experience; this is part of the evolutionary reward-learning mechanism we discussed earlier. Irrespective of whether we are consciously aware that we are looking forward to a situation, our dopamine levels will be raised. In the context of TNTs, this means it is extremely important that we don't let customers down by omitting the things they do expect or by doing them badly. Because when our prior expectations are not met, the inhibitory neurotransmitter GABA is released and sends dopamine levels plummeting. We feel this as the emotion of disappointment. So there is a flipside to TNTs too. When we do them they have an incredibly positive impact. But if we do not perform TNTs when customers have come to expect them, like being greeted by name or receiving signals that they have our full attention, there is a downside. This is why, for maximum success TNTs must be consistently applied. That was the real crux of our *swing and ding* analogy; not just acknowledging that elite sportspeople constantly modify and improve their process by making cumulative, incredibly small changes, but that through repetition and practice they make these small things a *habit*. They couldn't *not* do them even if they tried. Excellence has become their default setting.

I said earlier that TNTs have the power to disrupt; they allow smaller businesses to win customers away from bigger, better-resourced competitors. If you are a larger business, you have a lot to live up to in order to match customer expectations that have been set by idealised advertising campaigns and other outward projections of flawlessness. When you are a smaller business, customers may expect less and so it is, relatively speaking, easier to blow them away. I have no evidence to prove this next viewpoint of mine; but from everything I do know about people, customers and their expectations of businesses, *I believe dopamine may favour David over Goliath.*

I'd like to explore this by looking at a couple of examples of customer service; one from a very large company and the other from a small local enterprise. Both, bizarrely, involve car tyres.

Back in the 1980s, I attended my first customer service training course. As a measure of how seriously the company I'd joined took customer service, they had flown in their best trainer from the USA to teach us Brits *a thing or two*. It must have worked, because I still remember two things from the course. The first is that I was the role-player chosen to illustrate that the 2:1 ratio between the number of ears and mouths we have is also the ratio in which to use them; good service is about listening. However hard I tried to talk customers into being satisfied, it didn't work. I had to admit my trainer was right.

The second thing I remember is a story about a large Tokyo department store with greeters who bowed to customers as they entered and which had a customer service desk front and centre by the entrance, rather than hidden away on the 5th floor. According to our trainer that stuff was pretty standard amongst large Tokyo stores. What was unique about this particular store was its pledge to refund goods at any time if a customer was disappointed for any reason. We were told a story that one day a customer brought in a car tyre for a refund. The store representative couldn't find it on the inventory list, so had to ask the customer what they had paid for it. A credit was immediately made, even though the store didn't sell tyres and never had done. As the story concluded, our poor trainer had to endure 10 incredulous trainees protesting that it wasn't a great example of customer service, it was the greatest ever example of corporate stupidity. I still think about that story. Did someone enter Tokyo retail folklore through a mistaken refund? Was it a high-spending VIP customer? Perhaps store turnover was so high it could overlook gratuitous returns. Maybe this was the cost of good PR. Perhaps the story was even true. What I conclude today, with the benefit of nearly four decades of hindsight, is that it only proves grand gestures get publicity. Gestures affecting a handful of lucky customers aren't the same as trying to exceed the expectations of every single customer. PR stunts are part of the 'bling' not the 'ding'.

Maybe small companies are fortunate in only being able to afford to focus on the 'ding' of getting the little things right. Needing new car tyres last year, I ordered a set online and opted for fitting at a nearby industrial park. Unfamiliar with the location, I slowly drove up to some small premises.

Two people inside waved and smiled rather than staring; we were off to a good start. The manager confirmed they had my tyres, but apologised that I would have to wait for a fitting bay. Pointing at a vending machine, he asked whether I'd like a coffee. Quicker than I could check my pockets, the manager jumped up, put a coin in the machine and said: '*This one's on me – thanks for waiting.*' Of course, it actually cost him no more than the cost of the ingredients or the lease on the machine; he must take the coins out each night to use with tomorrow's customers. But that's not the point; it makes today's customers feel great. It was a TNT act of sheer genius.

A few months later, one of my new tyres got a puncture from a stray screw. I returned to the tyre depot and found another employee on the front desk who reassured me they could help. As I walked out to my car with him, he asked if I had bought my tyres from their outlet. Intrigued I said: '*What difference would it make if I hadn't?*' His answer took me completely by surprise: '*Exactly twenty pounds, as we never charge customers for repairing tyres we supplied.*' I was completely, utterly blown away. These guys were all about TNTs.

Think about it. If you walk into a fancy department store and they refund an expensive tyre, they might have met your expectation. If you go to a small local tyre-fitter and they offer you a free coffee or a complimentary repair, they may have massively exceeded your expectations. Which of these triggered the greatest dopamine release and left the customer feeling happiest? Which cost least? It is why great customer service isn't based on grand gestures; it just needs basic things done well, together with small gestures to show you care.

Somewhat appropriately for a tyre-based analogy, this really is a case of '*going the extra mile*'. Look at what your customers expect as the basics and make sure you do these consistently; every time and without exception. Then show how much you care by always taking those little extra steps that customers may not expect. It sounds so simple; and that's the thing about TNTs. In the main, they are really, really simple. Yet it continues to astonish me that so few people bother to go the extra mile. Why not? There's still plenty of space there.

There are no traffic jams along the extra mile.

Roger Staubach

I'd now like to highlight a further TNT opportunity; they are so powerful we should use them beyond our customers. What would happen if we started applying TNT-thinking to our interactions with colleagues, or in how we manage people in our teams? This TNT opportunity leverages another fascinating neurochemical fact. Not only do recipients of positive TNTs experience a surge in feel-good dopamine, but the person giving someone else a positive TNT will experience a dopamine blip too. Humans get an emotional lift from performing TNTs because our brains are built that way. We evolved as a social species; in order to encourage the collaboration and cooperation necessary for living in groups, our brains are hard-wired to feel good about both giving and receiving positive messages. People who receive a positive gesture, action or message are more likely to adopt positive-giving behaviour themselves. Sometimes, one person performing a single TNT can activate a chain reaction; a beautiful dopamine-driven, knock on effect. That's when TNTs become contagious; a feature managers can use to their advantage.

In **Cloud 7** we examine how leaders can foster team resilience and a workplace environment in which every team member feels comfortable being their true self, speaking up and knowing their honesty won't be held against them. It's a lot easier when every team member already feels valued. Using TNTs is a great place to start. Imagine if everyone in your team discovered the double-benefit of using TNTs to boost their own and colleagues' dopamine. The hours would fly by, the workplace environment would be one where people wanted to spend time; staff retention would soar.

You may be a fortunate manager who is confident that your team already knows that every interaction, with external customers and internal 'customers' or colleagues, is an opportunity to make a difference. If so, your job is simply to recognise and reward this behaviour; to show you notice and care when you see people making a difference. Whatever incentives you choose; from formal recognition schemes to a team pizza after work, any costs to your business are negligible compared to the competitive and commercial benefits.

However, if you're like most managers, you probably see TNTs happening occasionally, led by better or more experienced team members, but TNT use has not yet become widespread. What can you do to nurture this approach? No matter how busy you think you are, you must find time to help your team get to the point at which TNTs are so embedded that they are a habit. Where it is impossible for team members to perform any other way without being pulled up by colleagues. You'll then have reached the critical point at which TNTs are self-sustaining. In the meantime, you may need to stay more involved in day-to-day activities than you would otherwise choose so that you are hyper-aware of the dynamic within your team and close enough to quickly single out and praise examples of TNT behaviours as well as point out missed opportunities.

It also goes without saying that you should yourself incorporate TNT-based leadership actions, to set an example and inspire your team to follow.

Seven Fundamental TNT Leadership Actions

Listen with your eyes. When speaking with people, show they have your full attention by using full eye-contact. You would be shocked at how few leaders do this; with most distracted by taking notes, checking emails on their phones or reading through presentations. With the advent of virtual and home-working, videoconferencing is now commonplace. This same principle means you should not be tempted to turn off your camera; although you may be listening intently, the speaker doesn't know this. Eye contact is proven to enhance trust and rapport, allowing discussions to enter territory that could otherwise be off limits. It also allows you to read subliminal cues; for example, when you can sense there is something someone isn't telling you. If you are patient, you may find the right questions to draw this information out. On occasion, people tell me they are thinking of leaving their job when they haven't yet told their boss because the right conversation never happens. Tellingly, the reasons for wanting to leave are seldom big issues; they are often small dissatisfactions, which we might think of as 'negative' TNTs. If I was the manager of such an employee, I would want a conversation to explore how I could address their issues. It might start by simply looking them in the eye.

Don't give praise in passing. It's great when managers are motivated to give praise to team members and it's understandable and laudable that in our enthusiasm we are sometimes tempted to share this as soon as we see that person; whether passing in a corridor, sharing an elevator or standing at a water-cooler. It's far better though, to restrain that impulse; because praise given in passing is perceived by recipients as 'spur of the moment,' which dilutes the impact you want it to have. It is advantageous to be seen to go out of your way to deliver your praise or thanks as a planned and deliberate act. The impact is greater. Alternatively pick up the telephone or send them a 'thank you' note. Please notice I haven't mentioned email; just don't. And never be tempted to give gratuitous or unwanted praise just to be liked or get what you want. That's not using TNTs; that's called flattery and it's used to manipulate not motivate. Remember, people can smell the difference.

Don't just care, show you care. A lot of managers care, but unless they demonstrate it their team members and colleagues may never know. When researching my last book, I invited contributors to share TNT experiences that had made a lasting impact on them. What struck me amongst their stories of inspiring leaders and memorable colleagues was how small gestures could earn accolades like 'wonderful,' 'outstanding,' 'exceptional' or 'legendary'. Most TNTs involved modest actions such as stopping to say 'hi,' leaving handwritten notes, calls of appreciation, sending welcome cards or birthday cards, remembering people's families and tasty homemade treats being brought into the office. As well as many cups of tea being made.

Make it personal. There are some everyday TNTs that don't require much personal knowledge; for example, saying '*Good Morning*' or '*Goodnight*' to people, although this will have far more impact if you actually know their names. The most effective TNTs, however, are the ones that demonstrate how we value someone not just as an employee, but as a person. This means that we must be willing to spend time to get to know people, even if this has nothing to do with the business issue or project at hand. Social talk has a value. Some managers are naturally curious about people and need no persuading to get to know and understand how each person ticks. For others of us, it might be something we need to make an effort to do more. Knowing about someone's professional background or their family or their interests outside the workplace can allow our appreciation to be shown in small, thoughtful and highly personalised ways. People have shared TNTs with me where they were blown away by the fact their manager knew that they only ate vegan chocolates, drank oat milk coffees or were teetotal. They were overwhelmed by an appropriate treat, or by a gift that related to an outside passion or interest. How much more of a lift does a TNT give when it demonstrates a genuine interest in someone? It's immeasurable.

Be on time, every time. If you turn up late for a meeting, customers or colleagues may simply assume you are busy. That's why most people who show up late think they can get away with it. But what if teammates or clients suspect you are distracted, overwhelmed or they subconsciously perceive a lack of commitment; will they still want to work for you or with you? Besides being rude, being late is a demonstration of bad faith and I personally would question the probity or at least the executive skills of someone who is consistently late. I cannot be alone in thinking this way, so why would anyone take the risk of not being on time, every time? The same principle applies to always getting back to people when you said you would. You may lack a full answer but touching base to apprise people of progress shows your integrity. When you update someone that you have no new news, don't expect them to be happy. That's not why you do it; you do it because it's the right thing to do.

Your 'small' is a big thing to someone. If you're senior in an organisation, it's worth remembering most people only ever see you as a snapshot of your actions; not as someone who is as hard working and cares as much as they do. I was asked by the owners of a large engineering firm to address a precipitous fall in staff morale. It was clear after talking to workers that training wasn't the only thing required; they wanted something else. As a result of cost cutting, the biscuits in the crew room had been withdrawn. I was taken aback at the genuine hurt and anger this had caused; what management saw as a small overhead was a big thing to workers taking a break from long, arduous, hands-on shifts. I respectfully advised the owners to reinstate the biscuits; unsurprisingly, morale improved. Always be sensitive to, and prepared to act on, things that might seem insignificant or even trivial to you.

If you're going to be a bear, be a grizzly. I've always taken this unlikely quote from Mahatma Gandhi to mean '*if you're going to do anything, really go for it.'* There's a temptation with TNTs to stop after the obvious ones. That represents progress for many organisations and is probably better than most of their competitors, but it gets nowhere close to unlocking the full potential of TNTs. The businesses I see that are really flying on the back of a programme of implementing TNTs are those who have gone all-in; their leaders have become evangelists for TNTs and set the whole company looking at how TNTs can be incorporated in customer services, management training programmes, staff incentives and recognition schemes and even the office Christmas Party! When leveraging the power of TNTs, small definitely doesn't mean half-hearted.

I make no apology for the fact that nothing in the previous list is complex and some will seem like statements of the blindingly obvious. That's the whole point about TNTs, they are not difficult to implement. When I started talking to managers and businesses about TNTs, and even after I wrote a book about TNTs, I had no conception of what I would unleash. After I give a presentation, it doesn't matter what the key-note focus has been, the part that people are always most excited to ask me more about is TNTs. Each week I receive countless social media messages and forwarded posts from people sharing their own TNTs. If you search #TNTs you will uncover a community of people passing on their TNT experiences. I am humbled by the ingenuity of people's TNT ideas, in awe of how determinedly people are using TNTs to improve their businesses and astonished by their success.

Why am I, of all people, surprised? Maybe it's because TNTs are so incredibly simple and small that it's easy to forget how unbelievably powerful they are.

PURSUE MASTERY
TO FIND MEANING, SIMPLIFY
INTEGRITY, STRENGTH AND RESILIENCE
CELEBRATE FAILURE, LEARN FROM SUCCESS
CALMNESS, STRESS AND THE CHOICES WE MAKE

MY MOTIVATION ISN'T YOUR MOTIVATION

EMBRACE THE POWER OF SMALL
SEE PEOPLE AS THEY ARE
LET GO OF PERFECT

Cloud
4

My Motivation Isn't Your Motivation

Always remember that you are absolutely unique. Just like everyone else.

Margaret Mead

Once upon a time, I was fortunate enough to manage a team of salespeople in a fast-growing sector offering solutions most businesses needed. As you can imagine, if you understood the products and enjoyed helping clients, the sky was pretty much the limit for how successful you could be. As long as you possessed the necessary motivation.

I saw my job mainly as ensuring my team stayed motivated, which wasn't that difficult because once a couple of people at the company had a Bentley or a big house in the country, this alone tended to provide plenty of motivation for everyone else. This was, after all, way back in the 1980s.

Then, one day, I hired a young single mother to work in my team. Molly didn't have a typical background of sales experience, but she impressed me with her empathy for people and her sheer determination to land the job. After three months, Molly hadn't won a single contract; none of the incentives we offered seemed to make a difference. Since she clearly had ability, I sat down with her to find out if the issue was one of motivation. During a long and tearful discussion, Molly explained that, as she didn't want a Bentley or a larger house, she felt she didn't really fit with the rest of the team. I explained that to fit in, she didn't have to want the same as everyone else, she just had to do the best for our customers, which I knew she could do. Running out of options, I asked *'What would make you feel better about getting up in the morning to come to work?'* Molly's answer was immediate. *'A working Hoover.'*

When Molly had left the office that day, I cut a picture of a Hoover from a mail-order catalogue and pinned it in front of her desk. The next morning, soon after Molly got into work, I saw she had taken down the picture; perhaps my gesture of support had annoyed her. I let it pass; after all it was her private goal. Imagine my surprise the next day when I saw a different picture of a vacuum cleaner pinned up in front of her.

The following month Molly exceeded her sales target for the first time. In the months thereafter she beat her target again and again, accompanied by pictures of a microwave, a TV or a fridge freezer. I lost track and Molly went on to become one of our most valuable salespeople. She also taught me a priceless lesson; even after Molly had figured out that her motivation wasn't the same as other people's, the *vision* also had to be hers; it couldn't be *my* picture. It had to be *her* picture. Motivation must be *uniquely your own*.

Motivation, Inspiration and Enthusiasm

If had a pound every time somebody has come up to me after I've made a conference presentation and told me *'you have given me motivation'* then I'd be writing this book sat somewhere hot and sunny. These kindly intentioned audience members are as far from the truth as I am from a tropical beach. As I explained in **Cloud 1** I cannot motivate anyone except for myself. I can hopefully *enthuse* people by rousing the emotions of hope and self-belief, and *inspire* them by painting visions that they can use to set pictures in their own minds. But their motivation must be their own.

Many people confuse motivation, inspiration and enthusiasm; and use these words interchangeably. Although closely related, these three words do not describe the same thing at all.

Enthusiasm is an emotion. The word derives from the Greek *enthousiasmos*, which means *possessed*; making the point that emotions are our *response* to external events and interactions. The underlying components of enthusiasm include other emotions like excitement, hopefulness, optimism, self-confidence and eagerness to act. That's a powerful combination; but as I will explain soon, emotions are not enough on their own.

Inspiration is an action. When we inspire someone, we communicate about our own or somebody else's emotional state in a way that influences the listener to experience similar feelings and conjure their own emotions. This is reflected in the origin of *inspire*, which comes from a Latin word *inspirare* meaning '*to breathe into*'. I don't know about you, but I find that beautiful.

Motivation is something else entirely. The roots of the word come from the Latin *movere*, which means to disturb or set in motion. And that's the difference between motivation and inspiration or enthusiasm. Motivation describes our internal drive to create change around us. It has a force and a direction, and it is focused on very specific ends or *goals*.

In a straight fight between enthusiasm and motivation, motivation wins every time; one is a mere emotion and the other is a whole thought process. As we shall examine in **Cloud 9** when we ask the age-old question '*Why do we do things that we know are bad for us?*' we will see that many behaviours are determined by the way emotions and conscious thought processes interact.

Enthusiasm is similar to all other emotions in that it arises in our *midbrains*; an area including the *insula* and *periaqueductal region*, as well as the *amygdala*, which we met back in **Cloud 1** when we looked at why bad news stings most. Our midbrain generates all our emotions; our intangible subjective thoughts and feelings, and in order to help emotions serve their important evolutionary survival purpose of helping us learn and initiate actions, the midbrain has extensive connections with the prefrontal cortex, or forebrain. This large structure at the front of our brains governs a long list of functions, many of which can be summarised as our brain's *executive* or higher-order functions including maintaining and focusing attention and goal-directed behaviours.

It is a big simplification (but it is not wrong) to say that the midbrain governs how *we feel* about what we want, and the prefrontal cortex governs *how we go about getting it* through our mental representation and strategy. One promotes *enthusiasm*, the other provides *motivation*.

This statement is a simplification because we know other complex cognitive functions are shared across brain regions, so it is unlikely there is one brain sub-region solely responsible for motivation; and we have already noted that there is a neural super-highway connecting the midbrain and prefrontal cortex that share processes controlling our goal-seeking behaviour. However, it is broadly agreed amongst neuroscientists that the job of our prefrontal cortex is to govern functions such as *self-control, decision making, planning* and *problem solving*. That sounds like a pretty good definition of motivation to me.

And here's the bottom line. If you express enthusiasm for something in terms of how you want to *feel*; then you are still in the realm of emotion. You've just added new emotions to your original emotion of enthusiasm; for example, wanting to feel secure, successful or proud. These are all laudable but it means the whole thought cycle hasn't really left your midbrain. On the other hand, if you define what you are enthusiastic about in terms of tangible steps you will take, plans you will make and outcomes you can define or measure, then you have fully engaged your forebrain in the process; you have created motivation.

This is why dreams stay dreams, but plans can become achievements.

Please don't think I'm diminishing the contribution of the midbrain; midbrain processes are amazing in helping us live in the moment and navigate the complex emotional landscape that humans inhabit as social animals. I am a big fan of enthusiasm; it creates eagerness to act and it gets us up each morning to face the day's challenges with a smile. It's also infectious; our enthusiasm inspires others and we're lifted by meeting fellow enthusiasts. But whilst emotions are powerful and can inspire people to great things, we can't always control them. They have no direction; they have quantity – high or low – but no vector. Without motivation, enthusiasm lacks a destination. Without enthusiasm, motivation lacks a start point.

'Enthusiasm sets you on your way, but motivation gets you all the way.'

Goal Setting

In the remainder of this chapter, I'd like to look at the best tool we have for creating and sustaining motivation; how we set goals.

Although I believe it to be universal that we *should* set goals in order to support motivation, exactly *what* goals we set must be determined by each of us alone. Beyond the achievement of our basic needs for survival, our motivational drive is very personal and generally reflects what we want to become. External factors can influence motivation, like money, recognition, status and avoiding public failure. When you strip away measures of how we want others to see us, you find deeper motivations rooted in our internal sense of purpose and values; how we want to see ourselves.

That is why motivation is so deeply personal. You don't need me to tell you everyone is different. Some people thrive on motivation without showing much enthusiasm; they are driven, purposeful, highly efficient and possibly not much fun to be around. Others surf along a wave of enthusiasm, catching and inspiring many other people in their wake, but their motivation is typically more easily deflected. The truth is that we each need both qualities within us, and organisations – and book-writing partnerships – need both types of people.

When motivation is personal, it becomes powerful, resilient and not easily defeated. We fight hardest to preserve our sense of self. That's why motivation thrives on resistance; it feeds on challenges and becomes even stronger. Now compare that with enthusiasm, which waxes when progress feels effortless but wanes whenever it encounters obstacles.

Every year, on 1st January, millions of people set themselves a goal or even a number of goals; their New Year's resolutions. And these generally have a shockingly low success rate, because most people set themselves *outcome goals* rather than *means goals*. The distinction between these is absolutely critical and explains why most resolutions – and many other types of goals – fail.

Let me give you an example. I'd like to be 8 kgs lighter by the end of this year and I'm pretty motivated to do this, having achieved similar goals in the past. This is an *outcome* goal; it sets a specific target – which is a good goal characteristic – but it doesn't tell me anything about how I'm to get there.

To be sure of hitting my target, I need to figure out what I must do; my diet, what exercise I should be taking, behaviours I need to change. These are my *means goals* and there may be dozens of things I must do in order to be in with a chance of hitting my *outcome goal*. But if I do them, I am certain to make progress.

Means goals share the characteristic that they are small; none will get me all the way to my target. They are also black and white; I either succeed or I learn and try again. Lastly, they are very specific and relate to my daily and weekly behaviours. Each is individually achievable with a bit of self-discipline and effort, and every small achievement will give me a sense I am moving towards my outcome goal. Importantly, means goals can and should be modified as you find better ways to do things or decide you can do more; they do not change your overall target goal, except perhaps in bringing it closer.

Yes, it's harder work dealing in means goals. You need to plan in more detail, break the overall challenge down into its component parts and define strategies to control your behaviours that work against your goal. Luckily, these are all things your prefrontal cortex is very good at if you fully engage it. Outcome goals don't tax your forebrain so much; they are big and simple to conceive. And that's one of the reasons means goals work better: you start off with higher motivation levels *because* you made a bigger cognitive investment.

Outcome goals
- A single desired outcome measure
- Large, meaningful, all-encompassing
- Describes the 'what'
- Non-negotiable
- Linked to your overall business (or life purpose)

Means goals
- Multiple improvements and changes you can make
- Small, highly specific, and measurable as Yes/No
- Describes the 'how'
- Can be amended
- Linked to your business process (or lifestyle)

Set out like this, the difference looks fairly obvious. Yet you'd be surprised how many business managers I meet who only set outcome goals. Their instincts are correct, they want to aim high and think big; to hit an additional £1 million in turnover, open a new site or pursue a new opportunity. Their enthusiasm is infectious, which is why I love meeting them. But I often have to remind them that without articulating the small stepping stones of action-oriented means goals that pave the way, they and their teams will find it hard to hit their outcome goal.

I liken it to walking on bubble wrap (if you've never done this, try it!). Each step forward pops tens of tiny bubbles and not only do you feel buoyed by the sensation of literally walking on air, you have a sound-track of small exclamations to encourage you on. This is what it feels like to set and succeed at means goals. They mark progress, feed motivation and create momentum. Each time we hit them, more feel-good dopamine gets released in our midbrain, setting up a virtuous spiral of further enthusiasm and motivation.

When setting goals, whether in your business or personal life, the degree of clarity you have on whether you have outcome goals or means goals will hold the key to how successful you will be.

Doorstep Goals

The second-most popular question I am asked after 'What type of goals should I set?' is 'How do I know if I am setting my goals at an achievable level?' It's a great question.

I doubt there are many people in the commercial world who want to be accused of being under-ambitious. If you're running your own business, it's likely you have a strong desire for success; and if you manage a process or team in a larger organisation, it would be unusual if setting your sights high hadn't played a part in getting you where you are today. It may not come as a surprise when I tell you that many highly successful people I work with are over-ambitious, especially when it comes to goal setting.

You could view this under the category of 'it's a nice problem to have.' If you aim for the stars and land on the moon, then you've still achieved a lot. But the cumulative effect of continually missing goals can have a catastrophic, negative impact, on you and those around you. Repeated failure is extremely demotivating. Psychologists have calculated that the emotional impact of failure is around 2.5 times greater than the emotional benefit of winning. When people miss a target, it hurts 2.5 times more than it feels good when they exceed their target, even if it is by exactly the same amount in each case. In our minds, it doesn't average out.

You will recall from **Cloud 3** that, as part of our motivation–reward neural pathway, dopamine is released in our brains when we find an experience rewarding. This also happens when we achieve a goal. Remember also that our brains aren't that well-calibrated to know the difference between big positive experiences and small ones; and that dopamine is also released in anticipation of a rewarding experience. Taken together, these neurochemical facts would make a strong argument that it is more motivating to have cumulative small goals along the road to a big 'make or break' goal. It also shows why it is crucial that goals are set at the right level.

In my experience, people tend to set 'means goals' unrealistically high, yet may simultaneously set 'outcome goals' too cautiously. This is because people typically over-estimate what they can achieve in a day, week or month but under-estimate the cumulative long-term effect of the days they do achieve something modest. Even Albert Einstein had to concede that the human brain is not good at understanding the cumulative power of compounding over time.

So, what is the benchmark when setting goals at the right level? How do you find the precise point at which a goal is sufficiently challenging but not overwhelming? If a goal is too easy, it will just feel boringly routine; your motivation will rapidly become diminished and you'll become disengaged. Conversely, if a goal is too challenging then the chances are that you will find ways to avoid tackling it, knowing deep down that despite your best efforts, the outcome is inevitable. If you don't get your goal setting spot on, you'll either switch off or give up and whichever way it is, you won't feel particularly great about yourself. Motivation levels will fall, and you could end up finding yourself in a tailspin of disappointment.

The key to setting goals at an optimal level is to always remember that the reference point is not the quantity itself, but your own comfort zone. The ideal goals will be those that take you to the very edge of your comfort zone, but not wholly outside it. If your home represents your comfort zone, then I call this 'standing on your front doorstep'.

Let me share an example. Imagine someone who wanted to get to their desk earlier each day to catch up with emails, get ahead of their daily plan or read up on industry news and trends. If they already struggle to start at 9 a.m. then a goal of starting an hour earlier each day may be unsustainable. On the other hand getting up 30 minutes earlier every day, or an hour earlier twice a week, may lie just beyond their comfort zone and could, in time, become normal.

It's not just our routines and habits that make up our comfort zones, it's also our capabilities. If we find something intellectually demanding but not wholly impossible when we concentrate, then the neuroplasticity of the human brain will allow us to build new neural connections and learn new skills. If we stay in our comfort zone we won't learn anything new, and if we stray too far beyond it, we will struggle to stay motivated. If we are honest with ourselves about our own capabilities and we really do want to get somewhere, it is critical to bear in mind that every time we hit a new goal, we've expanded our comfort zone. Our front doorstep has moved.

Some 'tough' bosses believe that stretch goals rather than optimum goals are the key to motivation, but if those goals take people too far outside their comfort zone, stretch goals become counterproductive. For us and the teams we may manage, feeling as if we are making progress is essential to motivation. The key to keeping this happening is to set goals 'half a step' beyond your doorstep, just on the edge of your comfort zone. That's where the magic happens.

Internal and External Motivation

There is one further way in which people differ in their motivation. We have already acknowledged that some people's goals relate to how they want to be seen by others, and some goals are much more about affirming how we see ourselves. Psychologists refer to this as being either extrinsically or intrinsically motivated. As well as affecting the nature of our goals, this distinction can also impact why and how we drive ourselves towards those goals. Let me give you a very personal, but slightly unusual, example.

During the COVID 19 lockdowns, stuck at home and with gyms closed, thousands of people including me and many of my friends all jumped on stationary bicycle indoor trainers, or bike ergometers, in an effort to keep fit. Despite their various and different over-priced brand names, these devices all offered the same opportunity; to pedal nowhere fast and enter a whole new world of motivation and pain.

Personally, when I'm on my indoor bike I'm a fan of ride simulators; I go online, select a route and watch the virtual scenery pass by. You meet other riders; enter races or compete on timed sections to try to get on the leader board. It's also quite social and I like that too. I asked two of my friends which virtual ride software they preferred. Their answers surprised me, because people who also used a bike ergometer and who I thought were 'just like me' were not at all.

My first friend, who I will call Neo, puts sports TV on in the background and paces his ride by the numbers on his ergometer. Watts, speed, average pace and distance are his entire focus. Like Neo staring at the screen in the 'Goodbye Mr Anderson' Matrix scene, he just stares at the numbers.

Another friend, who I shall call Venkman, also rides in an entirely goal-focused way. Whatever his previous best; average watts or time over a certain distance, he chases the spectre of his own past performance until like a Ghostbuster, he captures this target and stores it for later examination.

How is it that three people who are performing the same activity choose to motivate themselves in totally different ways? It comes down to another level of difference between intrinsic factors and extrinsic factors. When you do something because it is personally rewarding; for the interest, enjoyment, satisfaction or fulfilment it provides – this is *intrinsic motivation*. If you do something in response to outside factors; such as receiving a reward, recognition, approval or avoiding disincentives that is *extrinsic motivation*.

Both types of motivation are important. Neither is *better* than the other and most people draw on instances of each depending on the context. But it is undeniable that some people are more extrinsically motivated, and other individuals are primarily intrinsically driven. Coming back to the three friends going nowhere on bicycles, why were there differences? Neo and Venkman ride against themselves. Their screen numbers represent targets that live inside their heads; this is intrinsic motivation. Whereas I want to interact with other people and measure myself by how I perform relative to others; that's extrinsic motivation.

I wasn't surprised to learn I am as extrinsically motivated in my leisure activity as elsewhere. I earn my living by engaging with audiences; coaching and training people and presenting at conferences. If I wasn't motivated to care what other people think, then I'm in the wrong job. Neo and Venkman set themselves intrinsic goals and it's not hard to see how an intrinsic model of motivation has shaped both their lives. Neo is, in real life, a former world-class sportsperson; internal drive kept Neo at the practice ground after the floodlights went off and nobody else cared. Venkman retired young to focus on other goals and it's not hard to see why he previously worked relentlessly to improve every tiny detail of the business he managed. In different lives, each of us found the right outlet for our own model of motivation.

To illustrate different models of motivation and the advantages and challenges each confers, I use a story I call *Lyre Birds and Show Ponies*.

Lyre Birds

If you think parrots are impressive, prepare to be amazed. Lyre Birds are native to Australia and out of all bird species have the most highly developed syrinx: the organ that allows birds to chirp, sing and call. Lyre Birds have the most complex mating call in the bird world and can remember a huge range of variations. They are such good singers they can mimic other bird species and can even recite songs from multiple different species at the same time. They can mimic other animals like dogs and reproduce sounds like cameras and chainsaws. One Lyre Bird has even been recorded mimicking a laser-gun film sound effect it heard on TV.

The most fascinating part is that Lyre Birds don't need to be trained or rewarded to mimic sounds; they simply have a strong internal drive to do new, complex things. This extraordinary ability doesn't seem to serve any biological purpose. Female Lyre Birds only respond when the male makes their species' call, so the extra repertoire carries no extra benefit. They simply do it for fun.

Show Ponies

Horses are amongst the most intelligent of all animals and their impressive cognitive abilities have long been harnessed by humans. Circus ponies and dressage horses are able to remember complex routines, synchronise sequences of movements with music and respond on cue to precise verbal commands and signals. Some performing horses can even carry out tasks that identify letters, numbers, shapes and colours. Horses recognise short words and are trained using repetition and positive reinforcement through rewards to promote their desired behaviour and develop their memory. Horses are also very sensitive to the emotional response they evoke in their trainers and human approval is just as important as receiving a treat to reinforce a horse's ability to retain and process information.

Show ponies and Lyre Birds are both incredible examples of sophisticated animal behaviour, showing how intelligent these creatures are. But there is *one key difference*: Take away the audience, the applause, music and trainer handing out sugar lumps; and the show pony stops performing. It won't step into the ring on its own. It saves its performance for when the external conditions and rewards are right; it conserves its effort and only performs when it really matters.

The Lyre Bird doesn't care if there's an audience because it doesn't notice. It sings in the absence of female birds, it sings without prompting or reward. It sings not because it can, but because it's incapable of not singing. You might say that's a burden as much as it is a gift.

If, like the Lyre Bird, you have an internal drive to seek satisfaction, fulfilment and even beauty through work, then you are in many ways fortunate. It is likely that your passion for what you do is all the motivation you need. But be warned, intrinsic drive is a cruel mistress that cannot be turned off. That's why the Lyre Bird still sings when it's alone.

If you are an intrinsically driven 'Lyre Bird,' you will need a job where you can exercise competence with a high level of autonomy. Task or target-based remuneration structures can be counterproductive for intrinsically motivated people since this may make them feel controlled by their work environment and become demotivated. If your boss is an extrinsically motivated person, they may struggle to understand you and motivate you towards their goals. Most importantly of all, when work brings its own satisfaction, you need a mechanism to help you step back and relax when you are not at work; with strategies to achieve a good work–life balance and avoid burning-out

Alternatively, you may be like the pragmatic show pony; saving your performance for when it matters and thrilling your audience by knowing exactly how to deliver what customers want and exactly what you get from it.

If you are an extrinsically motivated person, you need to ensure that the material rewards your job provides are in keeping with the effort you put in. If you feel under-rewarded by your salary and remuneration, or if you are denied the acknowledgement, recognition and status you deserve, you will become demotivated and your performance will quickly suffer. It is not wrong to identify that the conditions you need are not being met and to look elsewhere. In fact, it is absolutely essential to your performance that you do this.

I hope you found this slightly sideways glance at different models of motivation interesting. There is academic psychology research that confirms that intrinsic motivation generally leads to more positive task outcomes than extrinsic motivation; favouring Lyre Birds over show ponies. My own perspective is that, since we can't change which one we are, trying to determine which is 'better' is completely irrelevant.

The most important thing is to acknowledge that we are all different. If we can also figure out which motivation model we are; it's easier to find our way in life, collaborate effectively with people who are different to us and make others feel great about themselves. Then we can focus on achieving *our* success through *our* own motivation rather than trying to live up to someone else's definition. *Because my motivation is not your motivation.*

PURSUE MASTERY
TO FIND MEANING, SIMPLIFY
INTEGRITY, STRENGTH AND RESILIENCE
CELEBRATE FAILURE, LEARN FROM SUCCESS

CALMNESS, STRESS AND THE CHOICES WE MAKE

MY MOTIVATION ISN'T YOUR MOTIVATION
EMBRACE THE POWER OF SMALL
SEE PEOPLE AS THEY ARE
LET GO OF PERFECT

Cloud 5

Calmness, Stress and the Choices We Make

It is our choices, Harry, that show what we truly are, far more than our abilities.

Professor Dumbledore

Do you ever feel as if you spend your whole time reacting to crisis after crisis? I definitely do. And I dream sometimes of what it would be like if I could only slow my world down or, better still, hit a pause button. I'd be able to take time to see the bigger picture, think more clearly and make much better decisions and choices. And I bet I would be happier too.

In this chapter, I'm going to share some ideas for understanding and dealing with stress, and outline strategies to help us make smarter choices by clearing some of the fog that stress can place in our minds. It's as close as I've ever got to being able to step out of my world for a while before rejoining with a clearer view.

A passing theme in **Cloud 1**, which covered *negativity bias* and **Cloud 3**, which revealed how *dopamine* reflects and influences perceptions, is that *our brains evolved to deal with a very different world from the one we live in nowadays.* This is exactly the same reason why our minds and bodies are poorly adapted to deal with the complex stresses created by the modern world.

What Is Stress?

We have already met the *amygdala*, a small structure in your midbrain that processes sensory inputs and is very good at recognising threats and bad news. In terms of how humans deal with stress, the amygdala can be thought of as our brain's *'panic button'*. Once it has been pressed by a stimulus or experience we perceive as stressful, it initiates a stress response; a whole cascade of psychological and physiological responses that affect our minds and bodies. Our stress response is simply nature's way of turning up the dial. It is a mechanism that makes us temporarily stronger, faster and more alert and allows us to rise to challenges and deal with threats.

As we shall see later, it is important to understand that there are two component parts to our stress response; an immediate *short-term* response, and a *longer-lasting* component.

The short-term response involves adrenalin. When the amygdala sends its distress signal, the hypothalamus sends nerve signals to the adrenal glands, which sit on top of our kidneys, these then pump the hormone adrenalin into the bloodstream. Adrenalin increases your heart rate, boosts blood pressure and raises breathing and lung capacity. This classic 'fight-or-flight' response gives us extra strength, speed or endurance to deal with a threatening situation. As an evolutionary adaptation, it is quite literally a life saver.

The second part of our stress response is more complex. When the hypothalamus responds to the amygdala's distress signal, it doesn't only switch on adrenalin release; it initiates a series of hormonal signals involving the pituitary gland, which prompt the adrenal glands to release cortisol. Cortisol is another hormone with wide-ranging effects, including boosting energy levels and maintaining high levels of alertness.

This potent cocktail of adrenalin and cortisol doesn't just help us deal with extreme situations; these hormones in moderate doses are also beneficial to everyday performance. Cortisol motivates us and helps us focus. Adrenalin boosts our physical capability. Experiencing *some* stress is actually *good for us;* it helps us learn, build new skills and cope outside our comfort zone. Without stress, we'd lack the drive, attention and energy to perform at all. But constant high stress debilitates us and our performance suffers. *Why is it so hard to achieve an optimal stress level that keeps us performing at our peak?*

It is because, in the context of today's world, our stress-response mechanism is flawed. If our cave-dwelling ancestors came across a sabre-toothed tiger, it might attack or slink away. So, our response system evolved to switch fully on, and turn off completely when a threat passed. That's how it's *meant* to work.

Today's stresses are typically ever present. Unlike tigers, they don't slink off. Our work worries don't disappear at the day's end. Nor do concerns over finances, responsibilities to others or over-complex lives. We can't cope with continual stresses because our 'off' switch never gets pressed. In biological terms, our sympathetic nervous system – which turns up the cortisol – gets activated, but our parasympathetic nervous system – which is the off switch – doesn't get the signal it needs. So, when we experience sustained stress, our short-term response subsides and our adrenalin levels return to baseline, but our second, longer-lasting cortisol-producing stress response stays jammed on.

We perceive high cortisol levels through the emotion of anxiety; that's what hyper-vigilance feels like to our brains. It's why we can feel continually anxious. Worse still, if we worry about feeling anxious and picture the things that stress us, the primitive stress-response part of our brain can't tell the difference between imagined stimuli and real stressors; stress levels rise even more. That's *chronic* stress; our stress dial is stuck at 11.

Chronic stress increases risks of; anxiety, depression, digestive issues, low immunity, headache, muscle pain, sleep problems, weight gain and impaired memory and concentration. That's just for starters. Now the big ones; chronic stress also causes heart disease, heart attacks, hypertension and strokes. It may have been quicker to list how it doesn't kill you. If that doesn't persuade you how important it is to find techniques to deal with stress, you can skip to the next chapter now. For the rest of us, the first thing to do is accept that *some* stress is inevitable and *optimal* stress is actually good for us. Then make a plan to reduce *excess* stress. Realistically, you have three options:

Avoid – Could you remove or reduce regular stressors; finding the triggers and thinking about how to solve them? To reduce cumulative overall stress, you don't have to start with the biggest stressors if these are something you can't do anything about in the short term. Just start with ones you can fix. For me, it's supermarkets and rush hour commuting. Online grocery services sorted the first one. Years ago, I told colleagues I'd alternate starting work very early or after the rush hour, 'averaging' my start time. My headaches went, literally.

Reframe – You can choose to look at stressful situations differently by 'reframing' them. When other people's actions cause us stress, it is typically because we perceive their behaviour as aimed at us. But it isn't about you; it's about other people just being what they are. Remember 50 per cent of people are less polite or worse drivers than average. It's a statistical fact. So, if you get cut up by another driver, encounter selfishness or get insulted; think of a normal distribution bell curve. You just met the left-hand side. Reframe, and move on.

Defuse – There's no universal prescription. Deep down, most of us probably know what we could do to help reduce stress and lessen its unhealthy effects on our bodies and minds; exercise, healthful eating, proper sleep and relaxing socialising (as opposed to business socialising). A little of everything on this list is probably the best stress antidote. If you only pick one, choose exercise; just establish a consistent routine to avoid stressing over when to do it. Connecting with others is also essential; we evolved as an active, social species so our brains need activity and socialising to de-stress.

Some people defuse by using their parasympathetic nervous system to over-ride their jammed-on sympathetic nervous system. Activities like yoga or meditation initiate our parasympathetic nervous system and flick our sympathetic nervous system's off-switch. These activities work partly by helping us physically relax, which lowers our heart rate and blood pressure and allows us to breathe more deeply, and also by promoting calmness, improved mindfulness and emotional regulation, which directly reduce anxiety. There are many ways to capture a Zen-like mental state; choose any activity you find so absorbing that your brain blocks out everything but the present. Musicians, artists and writers know about Zen, but it can be found anywhere; playing sports, doing puzzles, reading, being outdoors. Researchers even proved that listening to audio apps of wind, water or waves instantly relaxes our brains.

If you are able to do any of these activities to counter stress, the most effective time is always whenever you feel the stress start. That's why the best solutions are ones you can use alone, any time. You must find your own Zen. I was initially sceptical; now it is a part of my daily routine.

Zen works because whilst stressful situations will always exist, the anxiety they trigger comes mainly from fear and uncertainty about future choices. Stresses from our past exist as regrets. In Zen you're only in the present; with the future and past put on hold, stress is temporarily on hold too. That's my pause button.

If you can combine any of these stress-reducing activities with an attitude of *self-compassion* you will be doing about all anyone can to deal with the stresses of the world we live in, without stepping off entirely. The next section looks at how to practise self-compassion; the best gift we can give ourselves.

Self-compassion

Learning self-compassion is one of life's most valuable lessons. As there are many viewpoints and theories on self-compassion, here's my definition:

Self-compassion is when we accept our weaknesses, flaws and insecurities and choose to respond by showing ourselves patience, understanding and kindness.

It is a lot harder than it sounds. And to have any chance of making this a habit that sticks, you should remember that the words above that matter most are *accept* and *choose*. Keep an eye out for these.

First, a question: If self-compassion is helpful, why is it that most humans don't exhibit this thought-pattern by default? I believe it's because in so many areas of our lives we are taught that self-worth is conditional. Schools value people on correct answers and exam grades. In our childhood we value ourselves based on popularity. In personal relationships we perceive our value in terms of attractiveness or appeal. And in our workplace, we are valued for our productivity or business or professional successes. We are surrounded by subtle and not-so-subtle messages about what we must be, do and be seen as in order to be of value.

We are not generally taught that we still have value when we fail. *So, when we don't succeed, we believe we deserve to feel hurt and pain. And we beat ourselves up, all over again.* This statement looks crazy; but it is true. And since this attitude is usually fairly deeply ingrained, it takes real conscious effort and willpower to overturn our instincts and start practicing self-compassion.

Step 1: Accept Your Flaws

Weaknesses, shortcomings, flaws – whatever you call them, we all have them. It's just part of natural human variation. So, accept them. Self-compassion doesn't involve believing you can never do anything to improve aspects of yourself,

and it doesn't mean inflating your weaknesses into a definition of who you are. It simply means you accept how you are,
and choose to focus on your strengths and those weaknesses
you can do something about.

Step 2: Deal with Now

Remember that the past cannot be changed, so don't keep
tripping over what's behind you. This triggers the negative
emotion of regret; you can lessen this by not being overly
focused on past decisions. Similarly, the future is yet unwrit-
ten, so don't make assumptions that will limit you. Accept
that everyone goes through challenges and any difficulties
you are experiencing are likely to be temporary. The only bit
you can choose to control is called NOW.

Step 3: Don't Beat Yourself Up

Everyone has an inner voice that focuses on negative thoughts
and emotions, fostering our sense of insecurity, inadequacy
or shame. It has been reported that we each have up to 80,000
thoughts a day; of which 80 per cent are negative and 95 per
cent are repetitive, so you are not alone. If learning to ignore
this self-critical internal voice won't work, try accepting any
criticism but reframe it in a more positive way. Think about
how you would choose to gently pass on your observations
to a friend in a similar situation, and use this blue-print to
replace negative self-talk with encouragement.

Step 4: Build a 'Win-or-Learn' Mindset

When you make mistakes, stop punishing yourself.
As we shall see in **Cloud 6** many breakthroughs, discoveries

and inventions were the result of errors. So, stop punishing yourself for your mistakes. Accept that everyone makes them from time to time and choose to look upon them as an opportunity to learn. After all, you've just eliminated an option by proving it doesn't work, which is a valuable piece of knowledge.

Step 5: Don't Care What Others Think

I'm not saying you should needlessly antagonise or offend others. But you should let go of your need for other people's validation; much of our negative thinking comes from how others perceive us and self-directed anger often stems from social pressure. When you choose not to base your happiness on outside influences you are accepting a final, huge act of self-kindness.

Did you notice the recurrence of the words *choose* and *accept* in every one of these strategies? That's because the act of acceptance and the ability to see that you have choices are central to self-compassion. Some people are uncomfortable with the concept of self-compassion, and others find that it is totally empowering and marvel that embracing our weaknesses can actually make us stronger. I hope you found something you could use.

I'd like now like to look at the single biggest contributor to the stresses we place upon ourselves when it comes to decision making. The reason we feel so overwhelmed by the number of decisions we need to take in today's world of limitless information and connected workplaces is not just the *volume* of information we need to sort through, but the fact that none of the technology that creates this volume helps us to distinguish the *important* from the *urgent*.

Important and Urgent

I've stood in front of a conference audience and been stopped mid-presentation and asked to explain the difference between *urgent* and *important* by someone who simply did not believe they were different things. It's a widespread misunderstanding; and I didn't mind at all, because that's what I was there for.

An example of something *urgent* would be a phone call from a colleague or friend wanting a favour. It triggers your emotional *urge* to react – hence, *urgent* – and whilst it's *important* to them, the consequences to you if you can't help are not. They're awkward – not life-changing.

Something *important* might be ensuring you have a periodic medical health check. It's not *urgent*; as it's not critical whether it happens next week, month or even year. But the outcome of never getting around to it may not only be life-changing it could be life-limiting. That counts as pretty important.

Some things of course are both *important* and *urgent*. Like when your health check is due and you've recently had some chest pain.

Put that way, there's a clear difference. But why do we sometimes struggle to keep this clearly in mind when we are struggling with the volume of information and decisions we are faced with daily?

It's because humans didn't evolve to juggle long-term and short-term priorities. If the tiger from the start of this chapter jumped out at our cave-living ancestor, the situation was both urgent and important. Humans lived in a world without distinction; when you survive season-to-season, driven by scarcity of food and a need for shelter, any task that needed doing – foraging, hunting, finding a safe place to live – needed doing now. The concept of long-term didn't exist; our brains evolved to rely on instinct.

If it feels urgent, then it's important.

Your Midbrain

That sort of mental short-cut is what psychologists call a *heuristic*; it's an in-built thought pattern that we are totally unaware of. This is a problem for humans in today's complex multitasking workplace and a further example of where our brains are ill-adapted to deal with the modern world. Even now, our primitive default instinct arising in our amygdala *makes urgent always feel important.* Unless we engage our logical forebrain to manage the emotion-heavy output of our midbrain, which is making us feel anxious and stressed, we risk getting so overwhelmed that we hit options paralysis and simply don't know what to do.

Luckily, there is a way to avoid options paralysis. Imagine you had a fool-proof strategy to differentiate between urgent and important; a set of questions to categorise any problem, a framework of clear priorities. Welcome to the *Eisenhower Principle* named after Dwight D. 'Ike' Eisenhower, five star general and US president.

I have two kinds of problems: the urgent and the important. The urgent are not important, and the important are never urgent.
Dwight D. Eisenhower

Ike famously organised his workload, priorities and daily activities around a matrix that classified tasks according to how urgent or important they were. There are now many variants on this theme and my own version is shown in the following matrix.

A – IMPORTANT and URGENT	B – IMPORTANT, NOT URGENT
Crises, deadlines and problems	**Planning, strategy, goals**
Require an immediate Decision or Action	Set aside protected time to focus on your priorities
C – URGENT, NOT IMPORTANT	**D – NOT URGENT OR IMPORTANT**
Interruptions, calls, meetings	**Requests, distractions, trivia**
Issues relating to other people's priorities: Delegate or Defer	Seriously, you need to ask? And turn off your social media!

You may have seen something like this before. Before we consider how to use this matrix, I'd like to share a word of warning around how *not* to use it. I have heard management coaches advocate the Eisenhower Matrix as a time management tool. This carries a risk that people see Box C tasks as easy and quick; so they think it's *productive* to address these issues first because they can cover a high quantity; by clearing their inbox, making telephone calls and answering questions. Sadly, these people are also kidding themselves. Great leaders know that *productivity* is not really about the *efficiency* of getting lots done; it's mostly about the *effectiveness* of focusing on exactly the right things.

Effective leaders focus on issues that are important, not just the urgent ones. To use the Eisenhower Matrix, simply list all your activities, projects and any other issues that occupy your time. Then, assign each issue, activity or project to one of the four boxes, by asking the following questions:

Q1. Is it important?
Important activities are tasks or decisions with an outcome that supports long-term objectives, missions and goals. If you determine something is important, it can be assigned to **Box A** or **Box B** depending on whether it is also urgent.

Q2. Is it urgent?

Urgent issues leave you no choice but to act, because the consequences of not dealing with them are immediate. There are two types of urgent: things that couldn't be foreseen; and work left until the last minute. Good prioritisation will always allow more time to deal with real emergencies.

If Q1 shows something is important, but you can't tell if it is also urgent, ask: '*Would a delayed remedy take longer, cost more or have a worse outcome?*' Use this answer as your Q2 answer.

Q3. What would happen if it wasn't done?

If Q1 and Q2 are both a 'no' then an issue is neither important nor urgent. Before putting this issue straight in Box D, you should ask what would happen if it simply wasn't done. Box D issues are mostly things other people want and Box D can fill up because we don't like to let people down. If your own goals and outcomes are unaffected and you are in a position to say a polite 'no' then leave the issue out of the matrix altogether.

With all issues sorted into their appropriate boxes, the following 'rules' apply:

BOX A: *Important and Urgent* issues sit at the top of your to-do list; you have no choice. Since you can't predict or avoid most unexpected issues, the best approach is to schedule time for unplanned events, and reschedule other tasks in the event of a crisis. If lots of tasks are urgent and important, ask what changes would help them to be foreseen.

BOX B: *Important but not Urgent* priorities need time set aside to ensure they get done; these provide fulfilment and success in our business and real lives. Highly successful leaders spend more time on Box B tasks than any other.

That fact should tell you what you need to do. It's hard to overcome our amygdala-led bias towards new and pressing issues, so the habit of keeping our focus on strategic tasks takes willpower and discipline.

BOX C: Urgent but not Important tasks prevent you from achieving your goals. They nearly always arise from the demands of others: interruptions, emails, phone calls and unplanned meetings. Ask yourself whether you can reschedule or delegate them. No-one wants to be a rude boss or colleague, but there are ways to encourage people to solve problems themselves. Alternatively, keep slots available for update meetings so people know when they can meet with you, and when not to interrupt.

BOX D: Not Important, not Urgent issues are mostly a distraction. Some business activity in this category could simply be cancelled; tasks may be a product of history, like obsolete processes or reports that nobody uses. If you are in a role where other people set your workload, it is more difficult to manage Box D since it involves turning down requests. If we are honest, some Box D issues may be pleasurable distractions. We must learn to set boundaries for ourselves and be firm about them. It's a matter of self-respect.

From experience, I know such tools can initially feel alien and mechanical but the thought processes quickly become automatic and you will find yourself classifying priorities without reference to the matrix itself; the classification system will exist within your mind. We should have been designed this way.

For me, there are two principal conclusions from the Eisenhower Matrix.

The first is that we must include making quality time for our friends and families as a Box B priority, which requires setting aside protected time. Without this ring-fence mechanism, it is simply too easy and too tempting to let this slip as other more urgent issues intrude on our lives.

The second is to acknowledge that the issues in Box C will probably be the most numerous and also the most challenging to deal with. The remedy here is likely to involve delegation; something which many people struggle with. I would like to close this chapter by taking a look at this important area.

Delegation, Ownership and Empowerment

I find it strange that the managers who tell me they want to cultivate greater ownership of issues and empowerment to make decisions amongst their teams are often the same people who complain their time is occupied dealing with urgent tasks. It's almost as if they haven't realised that one is the answer to the other; if they delegated their Box C issues to their staff or colleagues then they could achieve two objectives at once. But only if they delegate effectively.

Passing on the skills necessary to perform a delegated task is the easy part. *Show one, share one, ship one* is an expression used in medicine and probably elsewhere to describe a process of how you first demonstrate, then collaborate on, and lastly fully delegate a new skill or task to someone else. The key point is that, by the last step, you as the trainer have fully let go; and are not standing there checking over someone's shoulder as they stitch up a patient or examine a sore throat. It is this process of letting go that creates the positive sense of ownership and empowerment in a team member you have delegated a task or responsibility to.

I have found that most managers understand that they should demonstrate trust by fully letting go of the task they have delegated. They can deal with the need to ensure a good outcome, as well as manage their own anxieties, by agreeing clear definitions of the standard the task is to be performed to, the date when it will be completed and any review points along the way. Of course, a good manager will also reassure their team member that they are welcome to ask questions at any point along the way. But whether a manager does this effectively is not always an issue of whether they know how, it is deeply attitudinal.

As an illustration, I have a very dear friend who juggles a great deal in his life. He struggles to fit everything in and often beats himself up when he fails to achieve his goals. He could achieve more if he delegated, but he just can't bring himself to; he finds a reason to stay involved in every single task. When tradespeople come to his house to perform work, he literally cannot let go. He will stand outside chatting to his gardener, even though he knows he is preventing them from doing what he has paid them to do. When a roofer came to fix his tiles, he stood below calling out instructions even though he knew he was distracting someone balanced on a ladder at a great height. When someone came to maintain and install some programmes on his PC, he cancelled an engagement so he could be there looking over this person's shoulder. It's not that he doesn't believe they are all competent professionals; he just can't help himself and is incapable of dealing with his own anxiety in any other way than not letting go. It is his blind-spot; and like all blind-spots he is probably unaware of it as there is always a detailed excuse for why each case is different. If my friend had happened to be in Vatican City in 1512, he would have stood under the scaffolding calling 'Hey, *Michelangelo, do you think your fresco would look better with a bit more blue under that cloud?*'

The point of my story is that delegation is not an issue of ability, it's an issue of attitude, and it involves stepping outside our comfort zone. When our midbrains cause us anxiety, one response is to step back to our familiar habitual behaviours. This is the *not letting go* behaviour. An alternative is to actively engage our prefrontal cortex to design strategies that help us manage our anxiety by setting goals and a process that both we and the person we delegate to sign up to.

As I rose up the corporate ladder from office junior to more senior roles, I was ill-prepared to delegate when I was first promoted into leadership roles. I made every mistake possible. Looking back, I can see the answers were there all along. In fact, the solution was written in the title; like those TV quiz shows where the answer is literally on the screen but the contestant cannot see it.

Supervisor – you *supervise*, you do look over people's shoulders to check.

Manager – you *manage* staff or processes, not how people do their tasks.

Director – you *direct* people towards goals, and they choose their own way.

Delegation, the things I wish I'd known. Because done well, delegation is a sure-fire way to make other people feel great about themselves and what they do. Just remember to provide clarity about what you expect, then let go.

PURSUE MASTERY
TO FIND MEANING, SIMPLIFY
INTEGRITY, STRENGTH AND RESILIENCE
CELEBRATE FAILURE, LEARN
FROM SUCCESS
CALMNESS, STRESS AND THE CHOICES WE MAKE
MY MOTIVATION ISN'T YOUR MOTIVATION
EMBRACE THE POWER OF SMALL
SEE PEOPLE AS THEY ARE
LET GO OF PERFECT

Celebrate Failure, Learn from Success

It's not a failure if you tried, it's just success-adjacent.

SpongeBob SquarePants

There are many articles on leadership that urge us to learn from our failures, and celebrate our successes. And it's very good advice indeed. So why does my chapter title have *celebrate* and *learn* the other way around?

It is because, in this chapter, I'd like to explore a different way of thinking. I'm going to turn things around and look at three closely related ideas.

The first idea is that failure is not simply a trial or setback from which you dust yourself down and pick yourself up; although you must of course remember to do these things. Failure is actually a necessary part of a far-wider *creative* process; it shows us where the boundaries are, it builds our knowledge, it eliminates null options. And just occasionally, a mistake will provide a magnificent opportunity to take things in a whole new direction. Companies in cutting-edge industries like information technology and bioscience often structure their research and development functions as *incubators*; with the express purpose of *encouraging* failure. Multiple projects are initiated and taken as quickly as possible to the point at which they fail: in these highly competitive sectors, speed of learning is everything.

The second idea is that whilst innovation is great, most innovators fail not at the start of their process for want of a great idea, but at the end of their project or invention because of poor implementation or a lack of fine tuning and calibration. We will explore why the mindset required for the two processes of *innovation* and *calibration* is different and needs varying approaches. We will examine what you need to do to succeed at both.

The third idea is about an attitude. If great achievements are actually built on a succession of near misses, what would happen if we deliberately put ourselves far enough outside our comfort zone to find the very edge of failure? I am not advocating that we should deliberately court disaster, merely asking: *How much extra learning and success would accrue from being more agile and learning to live with our natural discomfort about unfamiliar challenges?*

Idea 1: Win or Learn

The opposite of winning doesn't have to be losing or failing. It can be an opportunity to learn. The expression '*I never lose. I either win or learn*' was coined by Nelson Mandela who knew something about overcoming adversity. Mandela understood that losing is not final; after you've picked yourself up, losing represents an opportunity to start over with the benefit of a little more knowledge next time.

This chapter is not going to presume to tell you how to apply this thinking in your own business or life. I don't know your business well enough, and I suspect you don't need me to tell you that everyone fails from time to time. Instead, I would like to share some great examples that illustrate and celebrate the *creative* possibility of failure. Here are 10 inventions that changed the world. Every single one of them, without exception, is the result of a *failure, mistake, error* or *accident*.

1. **Penicillin** Most people already know the story of how, on returning from holiday Alexander Fleming saw that in his earlier eagerness to get away from his laboratory, he hadn't washed his petri dishes properly. They had become contaminated with mould. Sorting through to see if any dishes could be salvaged, Fleming noticed that colonies of bacteria wouldn't grow around mould because of some unknown substance the mould was producing. From an act of scientific sloppiness, the first ever antibiotic drug was identified and millions of lives have subsequently been saved.

2. **Cardiac pacemaker** Wilson Greatbatch was a medical technician tasked with building an electronic heartbeat recorder. His mistake was to carelessly add the wrong value resistor to the machine's electronic circuit. When he tested the machine, he heard rhythmic beats coming from inside the device itself even when it wasn't wired up to a patient. In a stroke of inspiration, Greatbatch recalled that other scientists had recently told him that electrical stimulation could restore a damaged heart's natural rhythm. He shared his finding with colleagues who immediately saw its potential. An error led

directly to development of heart pacemaker implants, another life-saving mistake.

3. **Post-it® Notes** Spencer Silver's job at 3M Laboratories was to develop a super-strong adhesive. He failed spectacularly and invented exactly the opposite; a weak adhesive that easily lifted off. Silver himself saw potential in his discovery but it took over five years and collaboration with a colleague to come up with the idea for the Post-it® Note. Through Silver's mistake, vision and sheer perseverance, his invention is now used by millions daily.

4. **Celluloid** John Wesley Hyatt entered a competition to win $10,000 by finding an artificial replacement for ivory billiard balls. Hyatt failed to win, but he did accidentally spill a substance he was working with on his bench. When it dried into a thin clear sheet that was flexible and strong, he saw the opportunity for the world's first commercially produced plastic film, which enabled the birth of the motion-picture industry.

5. **Artificial sweeteners** Chemist Constantin Fahlberg was absorbed in working on industrial uses for coal tar, when he suddenly remembered he had planned a dinner with friends. He ran out his laboratory, forgetting to wash his hands. Later, as he ate a bread roll in the restaurant he noticed that it, and even his napkin, tasted curiously sweet. Realising that his hands had transferred the sweet chemical, he rushed back to his laboratory to identify which beaker held the sweet-tasting compound. He actually tasted them all; and named the sweet one saccharin.

6. **Microwave ovens** When engineer Percy Spencer was working on a radar transmitter, he noticed that the

high-power radio waves it produced had melted a candy bar in his coat pocket. As he cleaned up the sticky mess, he realised that it was warm and he saw the potential for this phenomenon to be used to heat food quickly. We have Percy Spencer to thank for all the hours of time the microwave oven has saved us.

7. **The Slinky®** If you're old enough to remember the 1970s advertising jingle 'a *spring, a spring, a marvellous thing*' then you will know the famous Slinky walking spring. This gadget was never intended to be used as a children's toy. Richard James was a US Naval Engineer who was developing stabilisation systems to keep fragile communications equipment steady on board ships. One day, he accidentally dropped a stabiliser spring he had made, and watched astounded as it 'walked' across the deck. A clumsy mistake gave rise to an iconic toy.

8. **Teflon** Most people 'know' Teflon was invented by NASA for the space race; except this version of the story is a myth. Its unusual properties were actually discovered by a refrigerator engineer named Roy Plunkett. Roy was involved in a project that was experimenting with new refrigerant liquids, in this case polytetrafluoroethylene, or PTFE. When he added this refrigerant to a test refrigerator it didn't work and the chemical seemed to vanish inside the fridge's pressure vessel. Curious, Roy cut the cylinder open to discover the inside coated with a hard, frictionless film. NASA did go on to use Teflon in space, but they didn't invent it. Roy Plunkett was the person who saw the potential when he made the world's most slippery mistake.

9. **WD-40®** This is my favourite example, because the story is quite literally told by the name. The Rocket

Chemical Company of San Diego was asked by the US military to develop a moisture dispersant to prevent surface corrosion on their missiles. The Rocket Chemical Company engineers had failed to find a solution 39 times before they found success with 'Water Displacement 40th Formula'; or WD-40® for short.

10. **Henry Ford** The motor manufacturer that still carries Henry Ford's name wasn't the first automobile company he started or even the second. Henry had established two unsuccessful companies already and had been written off as a failure by many. But with two failures behind him, Henry Ford had learned the valuable lesson that large-scale automotive production was only possible if he was also willing to adopt a radical new assembly-line process. On his third attempt, Henry Ford changed the entire course of industrial, manufacturing, economic and social history forever.

I hope you enjoyed reading these stories. If you want to foster a team culture where people are prepared to try hard enough to make mistakes and secure enough to put their hands up when they occasionally make them, then I hope these examples give you some encouraging ammunition to share. Younger team members may be especially reassured to hear you reinforce that we all have a choice in how we greet failure; we either let it pull us down, or we acknowledge it and rise up through what we learn.

Don't forget to share the real message behind each of these stories, which is not that a mistake was made or an endeavour failed. It's not even that a setback proved to be an opportunity in disguise.

The key message is the lucky coincidence that *each failure was greeted by a creative, enquiring and resilient mindset, which focused not on the failure itself, but on the opportunity and potential it held.* The world changed as a result; and that's why we should celebrate failures – they bring us progress. The next time you or a member of your team screws something up, remember: be there to help people shine *through* their failures; not *despite* their failures. Because you could be just one mistake away from your biggest success.

I would now like to move on to *idea two*; that innovation is worth nothing without calibration. If you are tasked with implementing a project that represents the culmination of other people's efforts, and you mismanage its implementation, then you have screwed up everyone else's good work and may be responsible for consigning an otherwise brilliant idea to the scrapheap. This is one area where I believe it is not permissible to make mistakes. Sorry.

Idea 2: Innovation and Calibration – Will Pareto Was Right

I don't have many heroes; I find the small achievements of everyday people made against the odds far more inspiring than towering achievements of great people. But I make an exception for Will (Vilfredo) Pareto who was one of the greatest thinkers of his time (1848–1923). Will Pareto was an Italian engineer, economist, philosopher and sociologist who invented modern quantitative economics and fearlessly embraced the doctrines of his sociologist detractors in order to find out why his abstract models didn't always work in practice. This remarkable man was more concerned with understanding why he was wrong than in showing he was right; it turns out his maths was correct but he forgot that humans don't always behave as rationally as he theorised. Ain't that so.

Today, we remember Will Pareto for the Pareto Principle or, as most of us know it, the 80/20 rule. At its simplest, this rule observes that any quantity is not distributed evenly; 20 per cent of drivers cause 80 per cent of all traffic accidents, or 20 per cent of your time creates 80 per cent of your happiness. In business, the rule predicts that 20 per cent of what you do will lead to 80 per cent of all outcomes; it is insightful to analyse whether 80 per cent of your overall sales, profits or customer complaints come from 20 per cent of products or customers.

When applied to most projects or goals, the Pareto Principle warns us that getting 80 per cent of the way towards an end point takes 20 per cent of the effort; and getting a project the last 20 per cent of the distance to the finish takes 80 per cent of the overall effort. Projects do not consume time or resource linearly; the last part is always the hardest. It was certainly true of writing this book.

To illustrate exactly why the end stages of any project raise specific challenges beyond their disproportionate consumption of time and effort, I'd like to share two visions I can never shake out of my mind. I love watching athletics and can remember races where a competitor, thinking they have a race won, eases up before the finish; only to be beaten by someone unseen and closing in. I've also been thrilled by close sprint finishes when an athlete dips their torso for the line too early, breaks their stride and is beaten by someone who stayed focused for a fraction of a second longer.

And here's the thing: I don't feel a shred of sympathy for those who came second. They had it coming. At the end of a race, the two things you do not do are ease up, or dip too early.

It's true too, about the end of a project. The difference between delivering a reliable working implementation or something that doesn't perform as expected lies in all the testing and fine tuning that is required. That's why it takes a surprising 80 per cent of the overall effort to get the last 20 per cent of the way. I call this final process *calibration*. The reason many projects fail at this final stage can be because people are tempted to ease up before the line, or dip too early. This is unforgiveable.

Innovate, Then Calibrate

To illustrate why it is so critical to get the calibration stage of any innovation process right, I like to use the following story.

Over 100 years ago, an artillery officer had the bright idea of using a new-fangled flying machine to see where his shells landed, and started a whole new way to fight wars. Aerial reconnaissance allowed you to see where your enemy was, their number and whether your ordnance was actually landing on them. In aeroplanes, unlike in balloons, which had been previously used for this task, you could get out the way if the enemy infantry fired at you, and choose when to go home afterwards. Because reconnaissance was equally valuable to both sides, aviators tried to prevent the enemy doing it. Pilots and navigators carried pistols in their pockets in case they weren't pleased to see you. But they seldom shot each other down; firing a small-calibre side-arm at a moving target whilst flying your own plane wasn't that easy; so, it wasn't that effective.

What was needed was a big gun, ideally a machine gun, mounted so it could be aimed properly. It was easiest to put a gun behind a pilot for a second crewman to use; but in that position it would point mainly sideways and backwards, which isn't particularly helpful when your enemy is in front of you.

It would be much better to point the gun forwards, in the pilot's eye line, so aiming is as easy as directing the aeroplane's nose at a target. Except the propeller is right in the way; the bullets would simply smash it to pieces. Or would they? If you've ever watched an aeroplane engine start, the blades appear to turn first one way, then the other; before disappearing in a blur. The feint blur is the blades, but it's mostly all the space between the blades. What if you could fire bullets through all that empty space?

When young engineer Anton Fokker proposed doing exactly that, people must have laughed or at least found it unlikely. Metal reinforcement plates to deflect bullets from propeller blades had been tried without success; Anton knew he needed a different solution. He took just four days to design an interrupter cam on the propeller shaft, with lobes to push a lever and temporarily lock the gun at the exact point at which each blade passed by.

The mechanism of this system is elegant and simple. The physics is not. Machine guns fire hundreds of bullets a minute. These don't arrive instantaneously at the gap between blades; there's a delay as bullets travel from the gun's barrel. Air speed, pressure changes and altitude will marginally affect the drag on bullets. In tight turns, a bullet's inertial path differs minutely from a plane's trajectory. These fine variances must be compensated. The mechanism must be calibrated by adjusting the cam profiles a fraction of a degree here or there, calculating tolerances, accommodating wear. One tiny error and – bang – the bullets eat through the blade and not the gap. Throw another chewed-up propeller on the scrapheap. The essence of this story is that innovation is great. But it's nothing without calibration. You can't assume that innovation and calibration happen hand-in-hand; it's eminently possible to get *innovation right* and *calibration wrong*. In fact, it's not just possible, it's likely; we know they are not natural partners.

In **Cloud 2** we looked at *working style*; how we all differ in being pre-disposed to be better or worse at particular types of tasks. In terms of our Cloud-2 skillsets, innovators and inventors are big-picture thinkers, generators of ideas and solvers of problems. They are likely to exhibit characteristics of *Drivers* who initiate, *Creators* who find solutions and *Orchestrators* who gather and organise resources. At the outset of a project, these are exactly the skills you need to get it off the ground and moving.

But as a project moves towards completion, it needs a different blend of skills; especially when it reaches the critical calibration stages. Late-stage projects still need problem-solving skills, but these are subtly different to the big picture problem-solving skills needed at the start of a project. Calibration is measured by the number of times you fail. It's painstaking: re-run tests, evaluate new routines, check alternative scenarios. Eat. Sleep. Test. Repeat. That doesn't sound like something you'd ask a big-picture thinker to do. In terms of our work-style skillsets, end-stage projects need an *Analyst*; someone with a careful, logical, diligent and data-oriented mindset.

When a company innovates, it normally puts the designer or originator of an idea in charge of a project. For most of a project timeline, this works well; *Drivers* inspire the team, *Creators* ensure a project stays true to their vision. But *Creators* and *Drivers* do not typically do follow-through tasks at all well. That's why, towards the end of a project, a different leadership style is needed.

If a project leader is brave, in the later stages they will pass across their precious project to be led by a different skillset. In the real world, this handover of responsibility does happen. Software companies, for example, spend fortunes on post-development testing and bug-fixing before products go live. Even then, they don't always get it right. When a bug stops your new computer game offering all its promised features, it's annoying. When your car's computer shuts down the engine on a motorway – that's more serious.

I'd shortlist shoddy software developers for a *broken propeller award* for poor calibration. On the list too would be people who design the hermetic plastic packaging for cheese, which looks great but you need an axe to open it. In first place, I'd put management consultants and business process re-engineering specialists; not all of them of course, just ones who do a bad job. When change programmes are done badly; it's typically not the initial consultation, scoping, process re-design, or systems specification that are poor. The shiny stuff will be brilliant. Where bad consultants fall down is in thinking their job is done before it is. They dip for the finish line, or ease up before the race is run. If they hung around longer as their clients got to grips with new systems in the real world, consultants could help with the inevitable and necessary calibration, rather than leaving their client to choose between work-arounds or re-designs.

If I worked as a business process re-engineer or consultant, I'd hang a shattered, broken wooden propeller on my office wall, to remind me daily that innovation is nothing without calibration. And if any of my team ever screwed up a client's business because they forgot that fact, I'd invite my project leader into my office to show them the propeller. Then I'd invite them to eat it.

Idea 3: Agile Comes with Fragile

The last idea in this chapter is about how our performance can be enhanced when we put ourselves outside our comfort zone. It's called a *comfort* zone for a reason; when we extend beyond it we experience discomfort from raised anxiety levels and we become more conscious of the risk we may fail. But there are also benefits. To explain these, I'd like to stay with our analogy of the lessons learned in the early days of aviation; starting with the very first day.

On 17 December 1903, just outside the town of Kitty Hawk, North Carolina, Orville and Wilbur Wright made mankind's first ever controlled, sustained flight in a powered, heavier-than-air aircraft. In just 12 seconds they made history, not only by flying; but because their Wright Flyer established a design blue-print that has endured up until this day. Their three-axis control system; with moveable surfaces on the wings, rudder and elevator to stabilise and manage pitch and direction, forms the basis for every fixed-wing aircraft since.

The Wright Flyer had one tricky handling characteristic; it was longitudinally unstable and the nose-up or nose-down attitude in flight was hard to manage. It turned out stability was improved by moving its centre of gravity forward; this became an important design goal to make early aeroplanes predictable, safer and easier to pilot. So, the Wright Brothers got it *almost* right.

Or did they? Within a decade, aeroplanes were being used in aerial dog-fights and pilots no longer wanted stable machines that turned and changed direction predictably and slowly. They wanted bigger control surfaces and twitchy aeroplanes that could out-turn the enemy. To gain in agility, they needed an element of longitudinal instability, so the centre of gravity in aeroplane design was moved back again, just like the original Wright Flyer. It turned out that the Wright Brothers may have been correct all along.

Nowadays, the latest generation of jet fighters are designed to be so unstable that no pilot could fly them unaided by back-up computerised flight-control systems. These deliberately unstable machines need only a tiny control input to complete a split-second manoeuvre. Just like 100 years ago, if you want to win aerial fights, the necessary agility is found right on the edge of instability.

This link between agility and instability occurs in other contexts too. You see this in elite sportspeople: a footballer running towards the goal, leaning at an improbable angle to outturn a defender, rugby players dancing at the limit of balance to sidestep tackles. All these examples show us that, if you want to push the boundaries of performance, you have to be comfortable with the idea of feeling uncomfortable, unstable, vulnerable, even fragile.

I'm not just talking about physical performance. Our mental ability to: learn, solve problems, develop new skills and perform at our best is enhanced when we have low-level feelings of anxiety, excitement, anticipation and possibly a little fear. In **Cloud 5** we looked at how the neurotransmitters and hormones associated with these emotions help us maintain focus, alertness and drive; and reinforce our capacity to learn. If we never experienced that daunting feeling of stepping up to the *edge of our doorstep* as I termed it previously; we'd never learn what we're truly capable of, or achieve anything exceptional.

If we bite off too much of a challenge, anxiety and fear might paralyse our ability to perform. But at the edge of, or just beyond, the boundary of our capability, we are right where our brains work best. *Neuroplasticity* is a term describing our brain's ability to respond to the demands we place on it by learning and adapting; it can reorganise neural pathways, make new connections and possibly even create new brain cells. And to *really* stimulate neuroplasticity, we must feel a degree of unfamiliarity, anxiety and challenge.

A common situation where I am asked to help people step beyond their comfort zone is in preparing them to make important presentations: either boardroom pitches, or public speaking to an audience. These are daunting activities for many people, but I have yet to meet anyone who hasn't improved through practice and experience. Usually, the biggest improvement comes from mastering anxiety, which can be achieved with a few basic techniques.

Overcoming Nerves

1. *Before you start, take deep breaths.* Not only will this stop your head spinning, it triggers your parasympathetic nervous system: slowing your breathing and heart rate, and calming your mind.
2. *Visualise your delivery.* Your goal is not to impress; it is to deliver a simple message, or explain a handful of well thought-through points effectively. Think about

how someone you admire for their confident delivery would approach the task. There can be few more effective presenters than three-time European Motivational Speaker of the Year Award winner Steve McDermott who explains how he once used a 'How would Carol Vorderman do it?' technique to visualise how to maintain a calm, relaxed style in a particularly high-pressure situation.

3. *Start slowly.* If you've ever run a marathon, you'll know the temptation to start too quickly. Presentations are the same: slow down until it feels *really* slow to you, your brain is working so fast that you perceive events differently to your audience. Then find your rhythm and pace yourself comfortably.

4. *Make it personal.* In a boardroom, sit opposite an ally so you can see a positive reaction. When presenting, pick a friendly face a few rows back; as you look all around the room, periodically turn as if you are pitching to that face.

5. *The audience has no script.* Most people worry that they'll forget points they want to make. This is odd; the audience has no expectation of the order you'll make your points in. If you slip up, they won't know – unless you tell them!

6. *Anxiety is your friend.* I've been presenting for over four decades, and I still feel a thrill of anxiety when I step in front of an audience. When I no longer do, it'll be time for me to give up. Anxiety and stress trigger release of cortisol and adrenaline; I think of these as legitimate performance enhancers. After all, drugs that boost these are banned in competitive sports.

I hope these thoughts have encouraged you to consider how you can become more comfortable about feeling uncomfortable. It's normal to crave stability; but when we want to perform at our absolute best, be agile, responsive and quick to learn and change direction, then we should go in search of discomfort. This is just one take-out from this chapter.

The next is to start viewing mistakes differently. The occasional failure is inevitable, and must be accepted. How you respond as a manager can take the brakes off the innovation potential of your team. Regard mistakes as success-adjacent.

The third take-out is that successful innovation will fail if implementation is flawed; particularly in the calibration-heavy later stages of a project, which require different key skillsets to those that ensure success at the outset.

So far, I have said nothing about how we should *learn from success*. What I mean by this is that when an initiative fails spectacularly, most businesses are quick to try to learn from failure. They will implement a comprehensive review to establish the root causes and ensure that it can never happen again. There is a business post-mortem or internal enquiry, reports are compiled, outside experts may be called in; people may even be sanctioned or lose their jobs.

However, when an initiative *succeeds spectacularly*, businesses do not typically hold an enquiry to establish exactly why it *did* work. Few managers forensically review the basis of their successes, putting the best analytical resources on the job and telling them not to stop searching until they have found every last cause so that it *will definitely happen* again.

In theory, we should be more highly motivated to replicate successes (which are many) than avoid failures (which are hopefully few). That is why a lack of desire to *learn from our successes* has always struck me as puzzling and odd. Great people can use both successes and failures as signposts towards further success and, in doing so, will make people around them feel more motivated along the way.

PURSUE MASTERY
TO FIND MEANING, SIMPLIFY
INTEGRITY, STRENGTH AND RESILIENCE
CELEBRATE FAILURE, LEARN FROM SUCCESS
CALMNESS, STRESS AND THE CHOICES WE MAKE
MY MOTIVATION ISN'T YOUR MOTIVATION
EMBRACE THE POWER OF SMALL
SEE PEOPLE AS THEY ARE
LET GO OF PERFECT

Cloud 7

Integrity, Strength and Resilience

You never know how strong you are until being strong is your only choice.
The greatness of a man is in his integrity and his ability to affect those around him positively.

Bob Marley

I love these quotes. To me, Bob Marley was the equal of any philosopher or poet. That's not to diminish his musical achievements; it's just my way of saying I don't think he gets enough credit for the way he saw the world.

In this chapter, I'd like to explore the qualities of *strength, integrity* and *resilience*. Like Bob Marley, the strength I'm referring to isn't physical; it's the *inner strength*, which comes from allowing our personal values to guide our behaviour. Our *integrity*, or to use a more old-fashioned word *character*, is the sum total of all the individual personal *values* we hold most important. You may not be surprised that there are very many of these values and, as a result, we are all individually different in *the shape of our integrity*. Lastly, *resilience* is a measure of how we maintain consistency between our values, integrity and our actions, even when we have to endure an enormous amount of pressure.

I will start by looking at resilience; since this is easily the number one topic leaders want to talk about when I am working with them and their teams.

Resilience

I am frequently asked how to foster resilience; how to forge the toughness in people that enables them to withstand pressure and adversity. This question always leaves me feeling slightly uncomfortable because although it is well-intentioned, by focusing on individuals it's starting from the wrong place.

A much better question to ask is: *How do we nurture resilience in organisations* so *that people can benefit from working in an environment that supports them individually and lessens the pressures they work under?*

And the answer is not as quick or easy as most business leaders want it to be.

The reason there's no simple remedy is explained by physics. Even if you apply infinite force, you can't stretch an object to eternity; you can only pull it so far. If you take anything beyond what's known as its *elastic limit* it's either going to snap, or it's going to lose its ability to recover its former shape. When the force applied is too strong, an object either breaks or buckles; its resilience is lost. When that happens to people rather than things, we call it fatigue or burnout.

The key insight is that resilience can only occur if tension is relieved *before it goes too far*. This is why boosting people's workplace resilience is far more complicated than you might think. Most individuals do not have the authority or means to change the factors that are causing stress on them and their colleagues *before* it happens. Resilience must be created at the level of the team or organisation, which can influence these stress producing factors. Organisations therefore need to think about what they can do to manage people's exposure to and experience of stress, rather than trying to make individuals more resilient. It's why the thing most managers say their teams need – *resilience training* – is a waste of time. Pulling people out of your organisation's front line to *teach* them resilience ignores the real issues. It is counterproductive because it results in the volume of work being temporarily spread across a smaller group; and depending on the messages it contains it may actually discourage those you really should be supporting and protecting.

I have seen resilience workshops telling staff that a healthy diet, sleep discipline, exercise and mindfulness activity can bolster energy levels and help them manage stress. These things are all true; but unless you match these messages with a commitment that an employer will also make significant changes to manage workplace pressure and improve their work culture, what these workshops effectively amount to is victim blaming. You are telling people that it's their own fault if they can't withstand the pressure because their lifestyle choices aren't good enough. They'll really appreciate that.

Before we look at the many helpful and effective things that leaders in organisations can do to help foster team resilience, I'll share some of the well-intentioned initiatives I've seen badged as *resilience support*; presumably in an effort to distract staff from the real issues. I've seen sofas and beanbags brought into offices, new coffee machines and healthy snacks, which quickly get discontinued. I've even seen scented candles. These are all nice things that no doubt help create a pleasant workplace environment and show staff they are valued, but when it comes to fostering resilience they are like putting a blister plaster over a fracture.

Seriously, scented candles? If you feel a need to set fire to something in your office, just burn all the victim-blaming presentation handouts. Let's look at some ideas that could make a more positive difference to people.

Resilient Teams and Psychological Safety

All the things that cause people stress in the workplace can be sorted into just two buckets. *Bucket One* contains issues like the volume and complexity of work, the lack of time to do anything properly, the insufficiency of budgets and resources, the ingratitude of customers and managers and the lack of reward.

In *Bucket Two* there is only one issue; the lack of influence people have to change, or even discuss, any of the issues in Bucket One. That's why so many people go home and moan to their partners about a whole raft of workplace issues they can't mention to their bosses.

Psychologists have proved that lack of *agency* or influence compounds stress. If people are exposed to stress and they feel they can do something about it, even if they can't do it immediately, anxiety levels are measurably lower than when they are exposed to the same stress but have no agency to change it.

If you want to reduce workplace stress and boost resilience, then help people see that they do have *agency* to contribute their ideas and change things. The first and most important step is to create an environment where all people within an organisation, however junior or senior, feel they can speak up, ask questions, give honest feedback and suggest ideas. Crucially, people must have the reassurance that, in finding their voice, they shouldn't fear being embarrassed, humiliated, side-lined or punished. In addition, everybody must share the belief that it's permissible to take interpersonal risks: to confront difficult issues and offer unusual solutions or ideas without being criticised. Managers must be authentic and open, take on suggestions from their teams and be prepared to drive change. Organisations must foster a culture of open communication. This shift in culture is so critical it has acquired its own name: *psychological safety*.

Despite the well-documented performance advantages enjoyed by teams embracing the principles of *psychological safety* – including better personal resilience – business leaders can misread its purpose. Some managers view psychological safety as an end in its own right, a box to tick and then move on. It's not: it is a permanent shift in the culture of a team or organisation in order to support people in working to their best potential. Other leaders only hear the word *safety* and fear that a *comfortable* workplace leads to complacency.

In fact, the opposite is true. Whilst increased psychological safety does make people feel included and valued, its focus on openness fosters vigorous debate; including on issues that haven't been confronted before. This is not comfortable. However, organisations typically report that if trust is developed, the catharsis of confronting long-standing problems motivates people to take ownership and solve them. As a leader, you must foster this *psychological safety* culture so that it percolates within your team and reinforces the other factors which can also be used to build resilient teams.

Building a Resilient Team

1. Remember Everybody Matters

Everyone in your team should know that getting the best out of each other means understanding that nobody is a nobody. No matter what someone's job title or experience, they are there to contribute something to overall team success, however small. Remember too, you may not have seen that contribution yet. So value everyone. Maintaining this attitude towards people isn't about who they are, it's about reflecting who you are. Above all, your role is to help people see each other's strengths. Team members must not only have confidence in their own abilities and skills, but also in the skills and abilities of those around them, especially if those skillsets are different to their own. Resilience is a collective phenomenon; people will experience less personal anxiety when they work as part of a team that believes it can collectively complete tasks that are beyond the scope of individuals. Training your team to understand their own and their colleagues' working style preferences is a building block towards a resilient team. When team members are on the same page about their own and colleagues' responsibilities and skills, then decision making and coordination are enhanced, even under adversity. Just don't call it resilience training.

2. Value Your Own Contribution

This one's for you if you are not the boss. You may currently be junior or less experienced; you may sit in a role you feel is not worthy of your talents. But using the expression '*I'm just a...*' when talking to other people is not helping them to value you. So please never start a sentence with these words.

3. Champion Your People

Be more enthusiastic about the people in your team and what they are capable of achieving than they are. I'm not advocating flattery, which never works. Just let your passion show and celebrate every team success and new opportunity, however small. Simply by doing this, you surpass most people's expectations of a manager or leader; your team will feel great and they'll want to spend time with you, listen and engage. That is a real gift and privilege that the majority of managers sadly never get to experience. Cherish it.

4. Make Sure Everyone Knows the Mission

When we believe in a reason why we do something, we find a strong sense of purpose and a willingness to go the extra mile and embrace necessary change. Think about the effort and sacrifice made in the COVID crisis by healthcare professionals. When I talk with people in these occupations, I'm struck that their resilience was tested not so much by long hours and scant resources; what frustrated them most was interference from people who simply didn't understand their mission. Your organisation may not be in the business of saving lives, but there is a laudable reason why you do what you do, in the way that you do it. Make sure you share this purpose with everyone in your team. Then ensure they know how much you value the part they play in doing it.

5. Encourage Risk Taking and Improvisation

If current procedures and processes hit capacity, telling your team to do more for longer, won't work. If you can't add resources, you must empower people to improvise and find new solutions. Most managers believe improvisation is random and to be avoided; but it can also be a deliberate process to adjust how situations are managed in real time. As long as teams reference past experience so novel ideas are based on more than guesswork, innovation will help your business to evolve and survive. You can support novel ideas whilst simultaneously running robust reviews to ensure quality is not sacrificed.

6. Review the Scale of Your Teams

Humans and their antecedents have existed for 6 million years, during which time they lived in extended family-sized groups. We are therefore psychologically comfortable being part of groups of roughly 10 to 20 people. This scale is large enough to allow diversity of skillsets and opportunities to learn from colleagues, but small enough that social bonds form and team members are supportive to and valued by colleagues. Big teams make people feel like a cog in a wheel, and very small teams may lack a group identity. Can larger teams be sub-divided, or smaller teams aggregated, in order to foster a scale where team members can be more mutually supportive?

7. It Must Start with You

Here's the big one. In building a resilient team, the biggest challenge to you as a leader is not how to implement changes to your team; it is about the changes you must also make in *yourself*.

To achieve any *lasting* change in the culture of your team, you must embody the very principles that you are trying to introduce. If you want to create an open environment that offers everyone a voice and the freedom to speak up, you must expect and allow them to be candid with you; so be prepared to not only hear but *welcome* feedback that you may not find comfortable.

The example you set directly influences how readily everybody else buys into the team vision you're trying to achieve. Resilient teams can only occur when absolutely everybody agrees, upfront, that this is what they all want. The destination must be decided before the team sets off on this journey. There can't be any dissenters trying to undermine other people's resolve as change will require a lot of courage from everyone on the team. They must be united; otherwise moving from a familiar way of working to something unknown will be too terrifying for some people and they will opt out.

As the leader of this change, you must be bold enough to lead from the front, but humble enough to show your team you are on the same journey as them. You will make mistakes, you will prove to your team that you are not perfect, and how you respond will be your single biggest opportunity to demonstrate that the principles of openness and honesty apply to everyone in the team. Especially you.

If you want to avoid the most easily made mistakes when leading a team, these are covered in our next points. They are:

being closed off to input so that confidence can become arrogance, and wanting to be feared or liked rather than respected.

8. Self-esteem Is Good, but Be Ego-Aware

We all have an ego; it's the part of our mind which links our conscious and unconscious thoughts and creates our sense of identity. Ego is not the pejorative term many people think it is; our ego helps us maintain a solid and healthy sense of self-esteem which is a positive quality, especially when we need to lead others. But there is a fine line between self-confident and arrogant. The difference is not one of *scale*; arrogance is not simply more inflated. Arrogance is being closed off to opinions and ideas; it arises when someone's exaggerated sense of their ability and knowledge means they fail to see how they could benefit from the advice of others. Self-confident people are secure in themselves and welcome ideas from others. That's the difference.

As we achieve success, our egos can blind us to this difference; we might not see it in ourselves. We may stop asking questions, solicit fewer opinions and become less consultative; not deliberately, but in response to the stresses and demands of being senior or running a bigger business. Leaders must be self-vigilant and not let their ego obstruct their view or, without realising, you'll end up clinging to outdated ideas and your judgement and decision making will not be as good as they could be. If we can't see this happening in ourselves, who can tell us? Our families and friends will; that's why we need a life outside the office, so we can remain grounded. We may have close workplace confidants who tell us what others can't or what we don't want to hear. Cultivate these relationships; and if you don't have any – ask yourself why.

9. Respect Is Trusting, Not Liking

Helping teams pull together and work effectively means getting people to trust each other and trust you as leader. The starting point is you demonstrating trust in them. Be open with your team about businesses challenges and priorities: this will not only help them understand why you ask them to do what you do, it will demonstrate that you trust them with important business information. Delegating tasks to people in your team is another way to show your trust; but only when you fully delegate responsibility for the task. **Cloud 5** looks at the *responsibility* and *trust* components of delegation, which must be properly transferred in order to empower people to take ownership of the outcome.

To gain trust in return, you must always be open and honest with everyone; not just transparent in your decision making, but open about your flaws and fallibilities. Initiating a discussion with your team about *working style preferences* described in **Cloud 2** can be a great way to foster this view. The one sure-fire way to get people to mistrust, or worse still distrust, you is if you try to appear as someone you are not. Teams do not expect their leader to be perfect: in fact, people are often drawn towards great leaders because of their fallibility; it makes them relatable. It also takes a lot less effort to be yourself; you aren't constantly thinking how to polish your image and conceal the truth. So be authentic: I would rather people disliked me for who I really am, than like me as some pretend person I'm not. I'm also not keen on being the butt of office jokes behind my back, which is exactly what happens to people who are fake.

Some managers confuse *trusting* with *liking*, and set about trying to get people to like them. This leads to the sure-fire secret to failure; trying to please everyone, all of the time. People who do this become inconsistent in their decision making because it is based on other people's wants, not what is right. They become seen as weak, easily influenced and lacking in integrity. Team confidence in them erodes to the point where they are not only distrusted, they are disliked. They have achieved unpopularity; the opposite of what they craved. Always remember, if you want to get the best out of people, you don't necessarily need them to like you, but you definitely need them to trust you.

10. Fear Is Not Respect

In **Cloud 4** we looked at motivation and why everyone's motivation is different. An aspect I omitted in order to cover it more fully here is the difference between *pull* motivation, which focuses on moving towards what we desire, and *push* motivation where we focus on avoidance or dislikes. Pull factors generally create better outcomes because they support a positive mindset based on emotions of hope and enthusiasm.

An example of *push* motivation is a failing student where shame and fear provide a necessary push for studying. However, once any exam is over the student is likely to revert to a habit of not studying, whereas a student driven by *pull* motivation of desired achievements will likely keep working. That's the downside; push-driven behaviour reverts when the trigger passes. What's more, since push motivation is based on negative emotions of anxiety and fear; it can lead to desperate, illogical and irrational decisions.

There is no doubt that push motivation works. Fear is a powerful driving force. So is animosity, humans evolved in competing social groups; our *tribal* mindset explains why we crave a sense of *belonging* in a group and why we define our personal and group identity by *what we are not*. Animosity is part of our psyche; giving people something to kick against can be a powerful motivator. Consider a group of military recruits being shouted at by a drill instructor. Shared animosity, even hatred, can unite teams, foster camaraderie and motivate people in highly challenging conditions.

Similarly, some leaders believe their teams are best motivated by making them fearful of the consequences of failure, even to the point of bosses enduring personal dislike in order to unify a group. It may work, but I wouldn't want to work there. A moderate form of *push* motivation is where rivalry with another team, department or close competitor is used to focus team effort in the same way that sports teams often have an intense antipathy towards local rivals. This was commonplace in two industries I worked in and, so long as people remember to see it as a business rivalry and not as anything more vindictive, destructive or personal, then this can be a useful technique to unite a team. Some people, and some teams, work better when they have an axe to grind.

Respect

When people I am coaching ask me 'How can I gain the respect of colleagues?' the answer I give is never the one they expect about *respect is earned and not given*. That is true, but it doesn't really tell us much about *how* to earn it. Instead, I explain that, like love, respect is one of those extraordinary quantities where – when you give it away – you can get far more of it back in return. Respect works like a reflection; when you shine it out to people around you, you will see it back. And the more respect you give, the more you will accrue.

A definition of respect I use is: '*to value someone based on their qualities or achievements*'. The word respect can be used as a *noun*, a quantity, or it can be a *verb*, an action. I deliberately chose the verb definition because people must choose to respect (*verb*) you; no-one automatically deserves respect (*noun*). The problem with knowing that respect must be earned is the temptation this brings to try too hard to earn respect. If you do this, people will only react to the *try too hard* bit and not the *earn respect* bit – which is counterproductive.

There is no secret to gaining people's respect other than understanding that when someone demonstrates respect for you, they are actually showing respect for the *authority* you represent. The type of authority I'm talking of here isn't the same as the way hierarchical organisations organise people by rank, grade, seniority, job title or even time served. Those are just labels. The authority I am talking about is your *personal authority*; it arises from your knowledge, expertise, achievements, enthusiasm, integrity, drive, reliability, commitment, vision, passion and compassion.

If you are a person with these qualities, you will in time get respect from the people around you by simply letting them see how you work; allowing them to see the qualities that underpin your authority. You must be willing to let them observe and understand the decisions you make, how you approach problems, deal with problems, cope with failure. This takes openness, authenticity and trust: by creating this transparency you are showing that you trust and respect the people around you.

It really is that simple. When it doesn't happen it's usually because someone is too busy or too inwardly focused to find time to share what they are doing and of course, to encourage, take an interest and show respect for what their colleagues are doing. If you hide the true you, if you don't give anything away, why would you expect people to respect you?

Integrity

In the introduction to this Chapter, I noted that *integrity* is broadly similar to the more old-fashioned notion of *character*. I tend to steer away from using the word character since although it does reflect our personal values, many people would also include in *character* some personality-based factors like behaviour, temperament and disposition. I prefer the term *integrity*.

The word comes from the Latin *integritas* meaning wholeness, which is a very good description of what it is: the sum total of the principles, values and qualities that are important to us personally. Notice that I haven't just said 'important' but 'important to us'. Integrity can, and will, be different for each of us. If you asked 10 people to define integrity, you may possibly get 10 different answers, which are highly likely to include:

Honesty	Reliability
Openness	Compassion
Wisdom	Humility
Generosity	Loyalty
Fairness	Respect

However, none of these are definitions or even synonyms; what we have instead is a list of ingredients. The way I like to think about integrity is that we are all a mixture of some of these ingredients. We differ in which of them is more, or less, resonant with us. The exact proportion will depend upon factors like the culture we grew up in, the influence of family and other close relationships, our experiences and also some innate factors that are just part of who we are. There is no *better* or *worse* combination: we are all uniquely different.

The Shape of Integrity

When I look down that list, I know immediately which values resonate most with me. I know which qualities I already possess; I know which ones I need to develop if I am to become the person I want to be. And I know the ones other people value in me. For me, there are four main ones – the shape of my integrity is a square. I don't beat myself up because it's not 6, or 10 sided. No-one's integrity is the shape of a kitchen sink with everything in it.

As another example, I have a close friend I admire greatly. He displays very little compassion or respect and his life revolves around the principles of loyalty, reliability and wisdom. He has come to know and accept that these things matter more to him than anything else when making big, important decisions. The shape of his integrity is a triangle.

My wife would be a five-sided star, and I also know a few six-sided stars. We cannot exactly choose which shape we want to be, but it is a helpful visualisation tool to understand ourselves and others. There is one other point to make about the shape of our integrity – the fewer sides it has, the less likely it is to get kicked out of shape. In other words, having a few values that we believe in very strongly will make it easier to stand up for those values under pressure and ensure that our actions match our values.

Strength

We noted in this chapter's introduction that our inner *strength* is what we draw on to ensure our personal values guide our behaviour; it's what enables us to maintain consistency between our values and our actions.

People can be strong in more than one way; different situations require different strategies and different strengths. Here's a story I use to look at different types of strength.

The Bamboo and the Sword

Ask people to imagine something really strong, and it's likely that at least some of them would picture a sword. It's a great metaphor for strength, that's why it appears in so many insignia, badges and logos. However, the fascinating thing about swords is that they don't start out strong. A sword was traditionally made of iron, a relatively soft metal. Think of an old-fashioned iron nail, if you've ever held one, you'll know how easy they are to bend. It doesn't feel much like the stuff that a sword is made of. But there's far more to sword making than there is to making a nail. Over centuries, different civilisations have perfected the art of heating iron ore to over 900°C, adding charcoal and working the resultant steel into a blade. This metal blade is then repeatedly hammered, folded and cooled up to 16 times; changing its physical properties further, adding hardness and strength. Finally, tempering the blade at 400°C adds toughness.

This is an apt analogy for how we develop strength and self-discipline since it is the basis of the expression 'forged through adversity'. When we endure hardship, it builds our mental strength and toughness. When we face difficult challenges, whether we succeed or not each time, we are nonetheless changed by the experience. If we get up again, we become stronger.

A bamboo plant is not as strong as a sword. But it has qualities that make it resilient. Weight for weight, bamboo is stronger than any other wood. When other trees crack; bamboo endures and survives by bending with the wind. Pliability, resilience, flexibility and endurance may not be types of strength that come as readily to mind as hardness or toughness, but they are no less important. In the same way that a sword gains strength by withstanding fire, a bamboo plant gains strength from withstanding an inhospitable environment. In ancient Japan and China, craftspeople knew the best, strongest, most flexible bamboo grew where it had endured the strongest winds.

Despite its strength, a sword can be fragile and snap whereas bamboo will bend and spring back undeterred. When we believe obstacles can be overcome without compromising our ideals, then we can be like the sword and confront. But if we need to spring back when we don't quite live up to our ideals, or if obstacles are too tough and we don't want our values to be broken by failures, then we should be like the bamboo. Great leaders help their teams understand that when we encounter challenges we can choose to resist and fight, or we can withstand and endure; letting our troubles flow around us like wind or water through a bamboo grove. That's not weakness; that's sometimes the greatest strength of all.

PURSUE MASTERY

TO FIND MEANING, SIMPLIFY

INTEGRITY, STRENGTH AND RESILIENCE

CELEBRATE FAILURE, LEARN FROM SUCCESS

CALMNESS, STRESS AND THE CHOICES WE MAKE

MY MOTIVATION ISN'T YOUR MOTIVATION

EMBRACE THE POWER OF SMALL

SEE PEOPLE AS THEY ARE

LET GO OF PERFECT

Cloud 8

To Find Meaning, Simplify

Perfection is achieved, not when there is nothing more to add, but when there is nothing left to take away.

Antoine de Saint-Exupéry

So far as we know, amongst all animals that show intelligence and can communicate, humans are unique in being able to construct and share *abstract* concepts; those with no direct representation in the physical world. These abstract thoughts are what we term *ideas* and in this chapter I want to look at how we create ideas and share these with other people. I'll look at how to effectively communicate complex ideas, and at how we can learn to apply *reductionist* thinking: breaking complicated ideas into their component parts, to draw profound insights out of apparent simplicity. First, I'm going to start by taking a semi-humorous look at what we can learn from how children think.

A highlight of the way I make my living is the opportunity it affords to meet extraordinarily successful people; to ask what drives them and understand how they do what they do.

Usually, they're people running businesses, but I also get to interrogate sportspeople, explorers and people who've faced extreme adversity. As well as feeling humbled and sometimes awestruck, I am constantly surprised how much high achievers from across disciplines have in common. There are eight basic ingredients that always seem to come up.

* They are extremely enthusiastic about life and have a real passion for whatever they do.
* They have bottomless reserves of determination, and regard failure, rejection and criticism simply as signposts towards success.
* They have a do-it-yourself attitude; rather than hanging around for others, they'll start having a go and ask for help if they get stuck.
* They favour action over debate; whilst others take time to scope opportunities and discuss implementation, they're already doing it.
* They have incredible mental and physical energy, which seems to energise and draw the best out of people around them.
* They ask questions; they have a genuine interest in the world around them and don't believe they yet have all the answers.
* They have a very clear 360° view of their mission and can explain it in a few, simple words.
* They usually know how to have fun, or at least derive pleasure from the process that underpins what they do.

When I first figured out this apparent 'formula' for success, I wondered how quickly these attributes could be learned and acquired by ordinary people. Then I became a father, and realised we don't even have to acquire them. Every one of us is born with all these behaviours already programmed inside. Look at the list – children have an abundance of every quality on there.

Child's Play

Imagine you're watching TV and a young child comes bounding in to see you: *'Is it true, is it really true we're going to the beach tomorrow?'* They stand there hopping from one foot to the other with excitement. You can't say no, and they can't think of anything but their single-minded mission to get there. They will immediately run to find their swimming costume; get on with gathering their beach toys. Their enthusiasm and energy levels are tangible, the questions start straight away; *'Will there be ice cream?'* *'Can we take the dog?'* They see no obstacles. It'll be fun; they can't wait. *'Are we there yet?'*

That story demonstrates every single attribute in our formula for success. Why can't we all stay like this as we grow into adults? It's partly because it's educated out of us: school happens. Before I get accused of being anti-education, let me say straight away that I'm not. Children need an education; today's world is complex and young adults need to emerge into it with the skills, knowledge and confidence to succeed. But it is undeniable that as we gain qualifications, somewhere along the way we lose our unrestrained energy levels, relentless questioning and our *'anything is possible'* belief. Rather than debate whether schools can or should preserve these qualities, I prefer to ask how we can rediscover these as adults. The answer, I believe, is to remember to look at the world with a childlike vision.

Start asking more questions As we become more established and senior in our roles, we can start thinking that our job is to provide all the answers for our teams. Not only does this disempower those around us and limit diversity of input, it stops us focusing on *asking* the right questions. Stay curious.

Seek variety and novelty Have you ever watched a child try to solve a problem? They employ a potent blend of logic, creativity and experimentation; simultaneously thinking their way through and around obstacles. I call this *corkscrew* thinking. One reason children's minds work as they do is because the barrier between their conscious and subconscious mind is less rigid. Psychologists estimate that a five year old uses up to 80 per cent of their creative potential, but by the age of 12 this has dropped to 2 per cent. To boost your creativity, seek new experiences and this will unleash your subconscious.

Don't be afraid to fail Have you watched a child learn to walk? They are basically falling forward using one leg at a time to arrest their fall. They show no fear, even though they repeatedly fail to stay upright. If we are staying where we are because we are uncertain of future success, then what we really fear is what others may think if we fail. You can choose to care a little bit less about this; don't be a prisoner of other people's thinking.

Keep learning As we age, we may lose the tremendous capacity of young children to learn new things; but we can still learn a remarkable amount. Even if what you learn relates to a non-work activity, the brain neuroplasticity that learning will promote can benefit all aspects of mental performance.

Boost your energy It's no coincidence that children rush around as they are absorbing and processing the world around them. The enhanced blood flow and neurotransmitter release triggered by all this exercise is directly supporting elevated cerebral activity. When did you last run?

Surveys of people working in large businesses regularly come up with the same set of words when asked what qualities they most want to see in their leaders. Results include: *trusting*, *authentic*, *challenging*, *questioning* and prepared to be *vulnerable*.

Wouldn't these make a reasonable definition of *childlike*? The quality of being childlike is not the same as being childish. It involves grabbing life with unbridled enthusiasm and never stopping asking questions. So be more childlike.

Icebergs

An aspect of childlike thinking that we could immediately derive benefit from is in being able to access the vast resource of our subconscious mind.

Everyone knows an iceberg is mostly underwater. Not so many know the ratio is 10 per cent above and 90 per cent below the water level. Always, no exceptions because whatever an iceberg's size and shape, it obeys Archimedes' Principle and the relative density of ice and water don't change that much with temperature or salinity. Now take a guess at what proportion of the human mind is occupied by conscious awareness, and how much by subconscious thoughts? If you guessed 90 per cent subconscious then I led you in the right direction; but that's still likely to be an understatement of the scale of our subconscious mental processes.

What is our huge subconscious for? Actually, that question is the wrong way around. The real question is why is our unique human consciousness so small? Here, psychologists do have an answer; if we were simultaneously aware of every thought we were having and every sensory input from inside and outside our bodies, we would simply be unable to process anything quickly enough. There have to be filters; some cognitive processes have to take priority. This is why there is a boundary between our subconscious and all the thought processes we are unaware of, and our conscious mind, which directs our thoughts and engages in abstract thinking,

This boundary isn't fixed and permanent; in fact you manage to by-pass this filter every night. Dreams arise from our subconscious mind; dreaming is part of the process of memory formation and our brains use dreams to re-order information and make connections between different ideas. Of course, we are mostly unaware this is going on and even the dreams we may recall are sampling a very small proportion of this activity. Dreams and subconscious thought processes are not just a sideshow or essential brain housekeeping. They are part of how humans solve problems. Have you ever woken and recalled a piece of information that had earlier escaped you? Or figured out answers to questions that defeated your conscious mind?

Amazingly, you don't have to leave it to chance and wait for your subconscious mind to surface and find you. There are techniques you can use specifically to boost your thinking by activating your subconscious and accessing its thoughts.

Dunking for ideas Thomas Edison would famously fall asleep in a chair holding two ball bearings and return to wakefulness when his relaxation made him drop them on a noisy metal tray. He found he could recall ideas prompted by his subconscious mind. If he'd had a smartphone with an alarm, he could have timed short 'power naps' and used a similar principle to enter the subconsciously productive hypnagogic state in between sleep and wakefulness. Even falling asleep naturally can produce great ideas, but you must remember to note them down before you fall asleep and forget.

Work whilst you sleep Here's a variation on the above technique. If you have problems you need to solve, especially complex ones; then 'prime' your brain by reading over the issue or making notes just before you go to sleep. The next day, you may find you have an answer or at least some progress; your subconscious was working on it. Unencumbered by logic it makes connections and sees things our conscious minds sometimes don't.

It's a swing thing Elite sportspeople can't leave their performance to chance. Repetitive practice trains their subconscious to control key aspects of their game, so it won't compete for mental resources with other second-by-second conscious decisions. Tennis players and golfers aim for 'motor automaticity' where their serve or drive is completely instinctive and controlled by the subconscious mind; they don't have to employ conscious neural pathways. The advantage is that these motor pathways are not impacted by anxiety or nerves. But we have all seen instances where players under pressure start to over-think their game, subconscious automaticity is lost and they get the 'yips'.

There are surprising ways you can use motor automaticity. For example, closing your eyes can trigger subconscious motor control. When I feel for a switch in the dark, I shut my eyes and my hand finds it. If I struggle to recall a guitar fretting sequence, I close my eyes and my fingers 'remember'. Blocking a dominant conscious sense lets the subconscious take over – even in the dark!

Heads or tails Why do we find it so hard to reach decisions? Sometimes it's about data. But if you get to a point where there is enough information and you still can't decide, there is a trick to use. Take a coin; assign heads or tails to each option. Capture your thoughts as you toss the coin in the air. Most people experience a *'Please let it be X'* moment. That's your subconscious talking: you'd already decided without knowing. It's probably not the best way to make your big life choices, but as a way to discover your underlying motivation it's a very useful technique.

Calmer karma Our subconscious has more sway over mood than we realise. If you feel stressed or want to enter a relaxed state to foster creativity and access your subconscious processes, you can use deep breathing exercises to activate your parasympathetic nervous system. This promotes physical calmness through reduced heart rate and blood pressure, and can also activate psychological effects including theta waves (patterns of electrical brain activity associated with hypnagogic, dreaming and deeply relaxed wakeful states).

MBMA When my team in a former role used to come to me with a problem they couldn't solve, I'd tell them they had become 'blocked' by applying the same thought process for too long. My suggestion would be to do an MBMA (*Management by Mucking About*). After 10 minutes of letting off steam by doing something ridiculous and entertaining, they would often return and figure out the solution that had previously eluded them. Their subconscious had somehow solved the problem as soon as they let the brakes off.

What all these examples show is that the subconscious part of your mind continually makes decisions without you needing to be aware. How much you chose to use your subconscious as a valuable hidden resource is up to you.

You may not feel comfortable using all the previous ideas and the Thomas Edison technique is fairly extreme. Not everyone is comfortable with meditation and breathing exercises. But do try some of them if you haven't done so before. My subconscious is literally the secret to my success; all my best ideas are the ones I wasn't trying to have, and I solve all of my toughest problems whilst I am asleep.

Keep It Simple

Have you ever noticed how some people make complex ideas sound staggeringly simple? Whilst other people can make even the simplest thing sound complicated; tying up their explanations in convoluted words and never quite getting to the point. It's because when you are confident in your knowledge, you're not trying to prove anything or show how clever you are, you're simply explaining. And as a result, you're likely to be explaining simply.

Simple explanations are partly about communication; sticking to everyday language, using short sentences and avoiding jargon – especially TLAs (three letter acronyms; sorry I couldn't resist). Simplicity is also about more than just our choice of words. Simple explanations also display clarity of thought, which doesn't just happen by accident when somebody opens their mouth and starts talking. Clarity shows that someone has sat down and *really* thought their ideas through first. They have rehearsed their thinking.

Albert Einstein famously said: *If you can't explain it to a six year old, you don't understand it yourself.* Whilst this sounds like a reiteration of the good presentation advice about keeping things simple and using straightforward language, Einstein was as you might expect also making a much deeper point.

The meaning I take out of Einstein's quote is that *the act of breaking down any explanation helps you understand, refine and improve it.* It is a skill to develop not just for the benefit of any audience who has to listen to your explanation, but for your own intellectual advantage in refining your own understanding. By dissecting bigger ideas down into all their smaller components you deepen your understanding of the relationship between all the parts; you establish which parts are proven facts and which are testable assumptions, you build links between cause and effect and you see how these relate to inputs and outputs. First simplify. Then simplify some more.

Why is this useful? Imagine you had to explain a complex business structure to an audience of customers, staff or stakeholders. If you started by showing the simple inputs and outputs of the business, and then the process steps in between and finally how the overall structure wraps around this; even a six year old could probably get the overall gist of it. I no longer have a six year old in the house, but I find it works fine to practise my ideas on my dog. She doesn't understand, but that's not the point. The point is that I understand that the process of repetition helps me question, refine and test my explanations until I have clarity and simplicity. As Einstein also said, 'Everything should be made as simple as possible, but not simpler.'

I'd like to share one further perspective on simplicity of thought, and this reflects the insight of yet another theoretical physicist, Richard Feynman. Feynman was a Nobel Prize winner whose brilliant work was only outshone by his ability to explain highly complex scientific concepts. Such was

Feynman's reputation that Einstein attended one of his lectures and Bill Gates called him '*the greatest teacher I never had*'. Despite pioneering extraordinarily complex mathematical models at the cutting edge of particle physics, Feynman's lectures were aimed at students with no specialist knowledge. One day, when Feynman found he was unable to explain a mathematical proof for the way a sub-atomic particle span in a way that an undergraduate could comprehend, he told his class, '*I'm sorry, I clearly don't understand it as well as I thought.*' Quite apart from the humility this displays, it shows that Feynman, like Einstein, truly believed that simplicity was the key to good explanations.

Championing the need for simplicity, the **Feynman Technique** describes the analytical process Richard Feynman followed and recommended to others:

Step 1 – When faced with a complex problem, start by listing, writing or drawing everything about the subject you know you already know.

Step 2 – Explain as if to a 12 year old using simple words. Remove jargon and complexity, which hide a lack of understanding. This finds knowledge gaps and helps you know what you don't yet know.

Step 3 – Reflect, refine and simplify. Go back to your source material, reviewing any parts you don't quite understand and finding missing information. Repeat until you have a simple, complete explanation.

Step 4 – Organise your ideas and test your understanding in the real world. Ask someone if your explanation was effective and whether any parts were confusing. Don't forget to review it periodically.

You don't have to have a brain like Albert Einstein or Richard Feynman to use either of these techniques. Anyone can refine and improve explanations as Einstein suggested, or use the four-step process set out by Feynman. These methods work precisely because they're not difficult. As you become practised in thinking this way, you'll not only be able to take your own ideas and explain them so simply a 6 year old or 12 year old could follow, you're also much less likely to be fooled by other people and their explanations. If you hear someone using jargon or complex terms; ask them to explain simply. If they can't, it's likely that they don't really understand; they just don't know that they don't.

The next, and final, aspect of how to frame and communicate ideas is how to apply *reductionist* thinking; breaking complicated ideas into their component parts. People are always talking about seeing the *big picture*, but they often misunderstand what is meant by this. Big doesn't mean *more* information or *greater* detail; big-picture thinking involves seeing *further*, by breaking down complex systems into the *fewest pieces arranged in the simplest possible way*. Big pictures are reductive.

See the Big Picture

One summer, I worked as a life guard at Virginia Beach. Before I was allowed to rescue people, I had to prove I could swim out to sea and retrieve a plastic buoy a few hundred yards offshore. It was much harder than I thought it would be. As a strong swimmer that bit was easy for me. However, I soon learned that strong currents would cause my course to drift and the wind and tide moved the buoy, so it was never where I saw it last, however fast I tried to swim there. In the choppy Atlantic swell, it wasn't easy to see my objective. I actually had to give up a couple of times.

When I tried a different technique, I made more progress. If I raised my head to keep my target in view I couldn't swim as fast, but I always reached the buoy more quickly. This surprised me, but not my trainer, which is why they had me do it; I had to learn to take time to look around and see the big picture.

Business leaders often ask me how they can learn to see the bigger picture, to step back and think strategically. Ensuring you have the right inputs is always a good starting point. Raising your head and getting an unfiltered view from staff, colleagues, suppliers and customers will provide a wealth of information; affirming what you already knew, and possibly telling you things you didn't. Listening to their concerns is valuable in itself, but in order to draw out ideas it's helpful to have some questions in your pocket. Explore each issue separately and be patient. Most people won't volunteer this straight away; especially if you're their boss. What you do next with this information is critical. It's likely this exercise will uncover some immediate actions. By all means fix urgent issues, but don't forget this exercise is about the big picture. You might at this point ask yourself whether your ability to *dive into the detail* of your business may be a distraction as much as an advantage. The bigger picture doesn't come from seeing more detail than anyone else; that's called information overload. Big-picture thinking involves seeing how things fit together. You need to let go of detail and picture a simple series of processes.

Science provides fascinating examples of how big-picture thinking transformed the way we look at the world. What we should learn from the examples given here is that, despite what science may look like, it doesn't celebrate complexity. The scientific purpose is to find the *minimum set of assumptions that explain something.* It calls out inconsistencies between what we observe and how others tell us things should be – it's disruptive.

Carl Linnaeus was a Swedish professor. In 1753 he figured out that every living thing on the planet could be classified based on similarities or differences. He arranged all 12,000 individual plant, animal, fungi and other species known at the time into a simple five-level hierarchy structure. Today, this system includes over 8 million species; with all known plants and animals organised into just 14 and 31 categories respectively. That's a massive piece of simplification and reductionist thinking that has yielded innumerable insights.

Dmitri Mendeleev was a Russian professor who designed a new visual representation of the 70 chemical elements known in 1871. Arranging elements by atomic weight, he saw they fitted a grid made up of columns of elements with similar properties. Where his pattern left gaps, he had the vision to propose that there were unknown elements. Today, all 118 known elements fit Mendeleev's *periodic table*, which still underpins all theoretical chemistry.

The takeaway from this short science lesson is that *people who were more than smart enough to deal with complexity saw that simplification was needed in order to move forward.* Big-picture thinking beats accumulation of detail.

Applying Big-Picture Thinking to a Business

To apply the principles of reductionist thinking, start by drawing the simplest plan of your business you can. Here's a model I've developed which you can adapt to fit the needs of your own business. Like Mendeleev, don't fret over any missing elements (see Table 8.1).

TABLE 8.1 Big-picture thinking model.

Input	Process	Output	External
Creativity	**Marketing** Product design Promotions Customer channels Sales support	**Sales** Market scope and insight Prospecting Bespoke solutions Relationship and sales channel management	**Customers** Review demographic and social factors impacting customer sales channel and segment models
Facilities	**Production** Product design Manufacture Quality control	**Delivery** Stock control Logistics Installation	**Technology** Monitor and evaluate changes in production technology including competitor adoption
Materials	**Purchasing** Supplier relations Purchasing strategy Inventory control		**Political, Economic and Environmental** Track factors that impact sourcing or costs of materials

MATERIALS   OPERATIONS   MARKETS

(*Continued*)

TABLE 8.1 (Continued)

	Input	Process	Output	External
PEOPLE	Talent	**Human Resources** Recruitment Staff management Training	**Manage Talent** Staff retention, reward and remuneration Support continuous training for front-line	**Competitors** Activity tracking Benchmarking Target recruitment
RISK	Counsel	**Legal and Compliance** Guide business Manage intellectual property	**Support Governance** Internal oversight Operating guidelines	**Legal and Regulatory** Identify rule shifts requiring process change to comply
SYSTEMS	Software and IT	**Systems** Design, commission or outsource IT and business systems	**Deliver the Platform** Systems and IT platform to support in-sourced business activities Manage out-sourcing	**Collaboration** Integration support: Alliances Joint ventures Buyer-supplier
MONEY	Capital and Credit	**Finance** Raise capital Manage credit Control costs	**Support Management** Provide and analyse key business metrics	**Financial Climate** Assess impact on banks, investors and other stakeholders

This may seem complex, but most businesses won't use all seven rows. Only three columns need information adding to them. As you fill in the boxes relevant to your business, think about where you can get data to track *process* and *output* activities. At a large company, data is likely to exist already. If you are a small or medium-sized business, you may be able to just walk over and ask someone, but most businesses are more complex than this and data sources may be disjointed or siloed in different departments or systems. If so, don't despair; even if you have to pull data together using spreadsheets, you simply need enough to answer one question:

What is the minimum end-to-end data that will allow me to spot bottlenecks before they happen?

In an ideal world, you'd spot issues from procurement to production, from sales to service; some companies can predict and solve issues before they even arise. But in the real world that most of our businesses operate in, you simply need to watch the pinch-points. To use a piece of unavoidable jargon, you need a minimum set of Key Performance Indicators (KPIs) that measure how your business is doing in areas like materials inventory, staffing levels, production volumes, product stock levels, marketing activity or sales orders. By knowing what your *normal* levels are and seeing how rises and falls in any one KPI could impact other down-stream processes, you'll have a pretty good big-picture warning system. You'll spot pinch-points and solve them.

The final component in this 'big-picture' model of a business is the information in the *external* column; how do you get intelligence on customers, competitors and economic and other factors affecting the industry or sector you are in? This is worth spending some effort on because it is where visionary leaders focus. They delegate the day-to-day running of their business to managers, so that they can spend their time looking outwards. Their big picture is bigger.

At this point, you'll have more 'big picture' at your disposal than most business leaders. Don't keep it all to yourself; when shared with colleagues it brings many benefits.

Communicate Better

Unclear communication is the surest way to create business chaos. This can be as simple as having unclear descriptions of processes, using different terms between departments or simply not knowing who to ask. Outlining business processes in a *touchstone* document ensures people see the same big picture and can work together more effectively.

Optimise Processes

If you have a head of Operations, the business schematic is a basis for regular updates. Reviewing KPIs shows if processes are working; initially to find the way to get things done and thereafter to fine tune and improve. Share this document at senior staff meetings; it will come into its own whenever you need to respond to internal or marketplace change. A shared view will help focus minds quickly on evaluating new options.

Ensure Consistency

Each business or team has a rhythm to which it works best. Laying out key business processes helps people find a reliable pattern and routine for their own tasks and understand how these relate to other functions. This promotes consistency and quality, and provides a framework for people to refer to if they can't deliver what is expected and need to flag up issues that may compromise dependability of results.

Demonstrate Compliance

Most industries are governed by sector-specific regulations as well as general legislation like data protection, health and safety and employment law. Breaches occur when deviations from company policy or standard operating procedure aren't recognised. If managers have a strong understanding of your business processes, it is easier to prevent non-compliant acts.

Out-compete Rivals

A business that runs like a well-oiled machine will outperform in its sector. Less money is lost to inefficient processes; capital is used more effectively, giving you financial resources to expand. Strong internal communication supports staff morale and retention to build an environment where people perform at their best. Your customers will see the difference in the dependability, quality and agility you offer.

Putting in all this effort to model your business and measure key processes may seem tedious and complex, but it leads to results. By making time to lift your head above the waves, benefits will be seen in every area. Your customers will notice, your marketplace will see you as the best choice, and your staff and colleagues will value the clarity you bring to business strategy.

But we haven't yet mentioned the biggest benefit. Your head-up focus doesn't just help you deal with cross-winds of competition, currents of change or economic or regulatory tides. It makes your day-to-day business simpler and easier to run. The time you liberate from managing business issues can be spent engaging with your team at all levels and helping them feel great about what they do.

In fact, your goal must be to continue to simplify your business to a point where even an idiot can run it. Because you never know – one day an idiot may have to.

PURSUE MASTERY
TO FIND MEANING, SIMPLIFY
INTEGRITY, STRENGTH AND RESILIENCE
CELEBRATE FAILURE, LEARN FROM SUCCESS
CALMNESS, STRESS AND THE CHOICES WE MAKE
MY MOTIVATION ISN'T YOUR MOTIVATION
EMBRACE THE POWER OF SMALL
SEE PEOPLE AS THEY ARE
LET GO OF PERFECT

Pursue Mastery

9

You have power over your mind, not outside events. Know this, and you will find strength.

Marcus Aurelius

S ome books contain a secret revealed only in the closing chapter. This book has no final exposé, but there is a concluding insight: the reason great people make other people feel great is because *they tend to feel better about themselves and what they do.*

This chapter explores why. It looks at the fulfilment we can gain through *mastery*; this is when people feel they are the architect of their own actions and they don't let impulses or emotions drive their behaviour or distract them.

When people are working towards goals, they spend less time debating whether to indulge in behaviours and distractions that don't align with their values: they exhibit self-discipline. Because they have a focus, they are more decisive. Since they feel in control, they are more satisfied with their lives. Consequently, they take more joy from what they do.

The Japanese have a *single word* to describe someone who has achieved unrivalled mastery over a period of 25 years: *takumi*. This may not surprise you, this is the same country with words for '*a person who looks beautiful from the back but not the front*' and allegedly for '*a man with a one sun-tanned arm*'.

The term *takumi* is reserved only for those reaching the highest pinnacle of proficiency. The word is written with the kanji characters *taku-* signifying *expand*, *open* or *support*, and *-mi* representing *good result* or *truth*. These origins reflect a deeper meaning beyond a measure of supreme skill or quality. *Takumi* describes a way of thinking and a state of mind. Like our word mastery, takumi describes both an *outcome* and a *process*.

The *process* of mastery uses sustained and deliberate effort over time to improve skill and knowledge until it results in excellence. Mastery requires sacrifice; it requires dedication of time that cannot be used for other pursuits. Mastery is the pursuit of perfection, but it doesn't require you to be perfect. This distinction allows you to celebrate the results you achieve as you develop mastery whilst knowing there is always something better to aim for.

If your endeavour is something you feel passion for, the sacrifice will not matter as you become fulfilled through your sense of progress. You may discover calmness through channelling your energies, liberating your subconscious and gaining self-knowledge by discovering what you truly think and feel. Some people also find a sense of identity through pursuing mastery; we are defined by what we make time to do.

The *outcome* of mastery isn't just the skill, expertise and knowledge you gain: it is the *mental qualities* you develop through the process. Have you ever watched someone perform a task over which they have complete mastery? Not only do they make it look effortless, they also manage to look as if they are enjoying it. They derive a quiet pleasure and satisfaction from their mastery. They look as if what they do completes them.

The *outcome* of mastery can't happen without the *process*. There's no short-cut. If you want to have what most people don't have; you must be prepared to do what most people won't do. This chapter breaks down this process and outlines the steps towards mastery. We will look at building self-discipline and willpower to overcome bad habits and make better choices. We will examine the purpose of mastery: knowledge, confidence and a sense of influence and control. Knowing we have made a difference is also important, so we will explore how to pass on knowledge and experience to others, completing the cycle of mastery. We all start as a student.

The path to mastery is often overlooked due to a conflicting belief that great performers are blessed with innate talent and natural capabilities: if we do not share these inborn *gifts* we cannot attain the same heights. I call this the *natural talent myth.*

The Natural Talent Myth

As I mentioned in Chapter 8, an interesting aspect of my work is the opportunity to meet some highly successful people. One thing that continually strikes me about such people is how little they put their success down to background or talent and how much is down to focus, effort and resilience.

Few came from glittering backgrounds and most didn't have huge talent as a youngster – although it's true some sportspeople and entertainers showed early promise and frankly it would be surprising if this wasn't so. The most important part of their backstory is invariably how they learned to cultivate and improve their own basic qualities. Talent wasn't born; it was developed.

I find that incredibly motivating, because *it's the exact opposite of what the media would have us believe.* Reports about sporting, artistic or other stars often tell us their talents arose as a result of special gifts and abilities, which, from birth, made them uniquely different to you and me. Well, it didn't. We shouldn't swallow the talent myth; we should ask why some people want to believe that if you don't have an innate advantage it's not worth aiming high. Is it because it provides a convenient excuse for anyone who never tried?

A common characteristic of high achievers is how they learned to master their craft through sustained, deliberate application and practice. They figured out early that our *abilities* have to be identified and worked on to become *talents*. I most admire those who were initially poor at what they wanted to do but didn't think, '*I can do nothing about it, it's just the way it is.*' They chose to think, '*I am where I am, but there are things I can do to get where I need to be.*'

Prove vs Improve

Whilst many successful people were undoubtedly driven by a desire to *prove* themselves, it was a relentless drive to *improve* themselves that led to success. If we accept this version of how success is achieved, it helps us realise two important things.

Firstly, if you focus on trying to *prove* yourself at every opportunity this is counterproductive to a mindset that fosters real improvement, which typically requires a lower-key attitude of humility, patience and a focus on personal improvement.

Secondly, repeatedly trying to prove you have mastered something you can't yet do well is fruitless. You will simply fail repeatedly until you lose motivation. Instead, you should improve your overall capability by focusing on a process that may involve a wide variety of skills. If you talk to elite-level performance coaches in the sporting, creative or commercial worlds, they mention both factors: *breadth of process* and *mental attitude*. A major sports science breakthrough over the past 20 years is a realisation that getting better at swimming, running, riding a bicycle or kicking a football doesn't require endless repetition of the same thing. Some sport-specific skills and techniques can only be developed in the saddle, pool or on the pitch; many other techniques are used to train speed, strength, endurance, resilience and cognition. When you put these together, the sum of improvements in many areas creates overall performance gains. This approach is well-established throughout the sporting world; why don't we split our real-world goals into distinct performance components, improving each in turn as we move towards our overall goal? Where is our process?

Mentality also matters. If you ask coaches to describe a performer they rate most, it's not always the spectacular superstars they pick. Often, they identify players or performers who are most coachable and reward training effort with the greatest gains; their mental attitude sets them apart because they understand the process and see improving as a goal in its own right. Such performers stand out because *improve mindset* thinking is uncommon.

For many people, the idea that our abilities can be split into component parts; isolated and developed through focused effort is quite alien. People may feel threatened by analysing their own capabilities, they may believe outcomes are more important than processes, or share the *talent myth* belief that they can't develop abilities they don't yet possess. Lastly, they may not want to believe improvement is based on disciplined repetition and consecutive development of skills because that sounds daunting and they lack the self-discipline and appetite for the hard work it entails.

I don't blame people for thinking this way. It's hard to break free from our conditioned beliefs about ability, talent and performance, but most successful people I know all have what I characterise as an improve mindset. Everyone has a choice to think this way and it is never too late to start: psychologists have demonstrated that as men and women get older, our orientation towards self-improvement actually increases.

There are five key differences between the *improve* and *prove* mindsets.

Cherish the Little Things

Some people think only big accomplishments are worthwhile: the grand prizes. But the *improve* mindset understands that momentous things are seldom gained by breakthroughs. They are achieved by painstaking, meticulous application of unseen efforts towards a thousand small goals; through consistency, focus, tenacity and an unwavering belief in the value of a process that turns multiple tiny gains into a substantial overall gain.

Understand That Everything Is a Work in Progress

People with a *prove* mindset think achieving their desires will allow them to sit back and enjoy the fruits of their achievement. In reality, the world moves on and no single achievement creates lasting fulfilment. It is easier for people with an *improve* mentality to feel fulfilled because they understand that success is a journey not a destination and they learn to enjoy the process and the sense of purpose and small achievements it brings. The key to happiness is progress.

Greet Feedback and Criticism as Signposts

The *prove* mindset resents and avoids feedback because it is primarily focused on status and can't accept messages that contradict this self-view. Such people tend to take criticism personally and challenge its validity. An *improve* mindset will graciously accept and even solicit feedback because they see value in criticism that can become actionable learning and development.

Confident People Have Less to Prove

Imagine you had to constantly prove yourself, seeking everyone's validation before you could feel good about yourself. It would be so exhausting you'd have no time to actually achieve anything. The *improve* mindset provides an alternative focus on small steps towards progress, allowing you to base your self-worth on your honest assessment of how you are progressing; self-esteem is not based on how you are perceived by others.

Praise What People Do

If you are in a position of leadership and want to encourage your team to focus on *improve* rather than *prove*, ensure feedback acknowledges and rewards behaviours like focus, tenacity and resilience as well as recognising goal achievement. Never praise qualities that cannot be developed by others. It's great if you have high IQ people in your team but they don't deserve praise for this any more than for their shoe size. Instead, praise them for what they do.

Steps Towards Mastery

Now that we have debunked the talent myth and established that talented people attribute success to the disciplined pursuit of skills and thought processes necessary for achieving mastery, what can we learn about ourselves?

The first point to note is that mastery is only achieved if we are not deflected by emotional responses to life's challenges. It requires maturity to resist our instincts and urges, and then make calm choices.

When we are young, we have no mastery, we cannot see beyond our own immediate needs and desires; as we get older this changes. By the time we leave childhood, we've learned how to deal with rejections, setbacks, obstacles and challenges. We have learned to master our emotions to a degree, which is helpful in coping with tasks we don't like, bosses we could strangle, the rudeness of strangers and life's general unfairness. But it's likely that deep down, our emotions are still driving our habits and behaviours in ways we cannot see. In order to achieve mastery, we need to challenge this.

Habitual Behaviour and Self-discipline

Why can't we change our bad habits? It's a conundrum that's frustrated mankind since the philosophers of Greece and Rome noted that we continue to do things we know are bad for us.

In **Cloud 5** we looked at why humans are bad at telling important from urgent, but this only partly explains why we sacrifice what is *important* for what we want *now*. Humans solve complex problems, understand cause and effect, and balance the costs and benefits of actions; our problem is not lack of intellect. If we know that too many alcoholic drinks, snacking on junk food or spending money we don't have are bad for us, why are we tempted?

As we noted in previous chapters, our brain was formed by evolution long before we became modern humans. Back then, satisfying immediate needs by having what we want *now* wasn't a bad strategy; our ancestors lived in a world of scarce food and deadly threats. Since the odds against successfully reproducing were not good, our brains developed powerful drives to seek food, resources and mating opportunities: to try to turn the odds in our favour. If you found food, you ate it all. If you found more, you ate that as well because your next meal might be a long time coming.

Clearly it worked: humans survived. But because of how our survival-seeking brain still works, we now face temptations our brain isn't evolved to manage. We must learn strategies to manage our behaviour. To explain, I must start with an anatomy lesson. Our brain can be thought of as including three bits:

The base of our brain is called the **brain stem**. This governs basic life functions like regulating our heart, breathing and sleep. Although affected by conscious inputs, brain stem actions are automatic and we are unaware of them.

The **midbrain** is where things get interesting. This contains complex functions including the limbic system, which creates our capacity for emotion, memory and motivation. This part of the brain drives activities important for survival, such as distinguishing good from bad, food vs predator, safety vs threat. We aren't designed to pause and think about responses; behaviours are automatic and rewarded with release of dopamine, which we met in **Clouds 3 and 4** and which makes us feel pleasure and satisfaction. So, we learn to perform these behaviours again, and again. This is the habit-forming part of our brain.

The third part, the **forebrain** and **prefrontal cortex**, is the bit we typically think of when ask, '*what does your brain do?*' The prefrontal cortex governs rational thinking, reasoning, conscious decision making and creativity amongst other things. It is where our unique human mental abilities arise.

These three brain areas don't exist in isolation, they are interconnected. The brain stem is under partial control from other brain regions and the midbrain and prefrontal cortex affect each other. All these brain areas contain cells called neurons, there are billions of them and they can consume energy at an astonishing rate. To conserve energy, the brain evolved to become very energy efficient by working only when it has to. The brain stem is *always on*; even when asleep we must control our temperature, heart rate and breathing. The midbrain can be thought of as *always on* if we are awake; when we are aware of its impact on our emotions or sensations like hunger. The forebrain does something very different: neurons in the prefrontal cortex can use more energy than muscle cells when you're concentrating really hard, so parts of the prefrontal cortex are designed to work *only on-demand*, activated when we choose to focus attention on a particular thought process.

If habitual behaviour is driven by urges, impulses and behaviours initiated by our *always on* midbrain limbic system, and the prefrontal cortex, which we use to resist these urges, may be on *standby mode*, that's a pretty significant evolutionary design flaw. What's more our brain's flawed design doesn't just apply to its neural hardware, but to its programming too. Because the limbic system evolved to ensure survival, its default setting is *stick to what worked before*; it repeats behaviours with outcomes that prompt a dopamine burst. Repeat behaviours are habits. In evolutionary terms, habits ensure survival; they result in quick, highly efficient, consistent responses and become automatic, requiring low cognitive effort.

Eating when we're not hungry and conserving energy by resting had evolutionary value so both became repeat behaviours driven and rewarded by our limbic system. Our midbrain generates an endless stream of desire for habitual gratification; not all desires are bad for us, but some habits are and they are hard to resist. When we try to shift habitual behaviour, the limbic system signals that it wants to revert to its previous 'default' setting by triggering emotions like anxiety, low mood or fear. Since habits we perform most frequently form the strongest automatic neural pathways, changing a long-standing behaviour results in considerable mental discomfort. If you've tried to change a habit, you'll know this.

There are two ways to beat a habit. You either *displace* the habitual behaviour with a less harmful alternative, or you *replace* the underlying motivational drive with a desire to achieve something different. The strategies sound similar but to your brain they are different: one modifies a behaviour's effect whereas the other addresses the cause.

Let me give you an example. When preparing presentations, I find myself periodically wandering into the kitchen to round up any stray biscuits. I tell myself I deserve a treat for working hard: a reward, a shot of dopamine, the rush of blood sugar; but substituting a healthy snack will do me more good. I haven't changed the underlying emotional driver, and consequently I haven't changed my reward-seeking behaviour, but by choosing healthier snacks I've lessened its harm. I'm not criticising this approach. For many people it works, and whole industries exist to help us displace habits: with cigarette-alternatives, alcohol-free drinks and lower sugar snacks. Equally, these industries keep us hooked on gratifying our immediate needs, just in a less harmful way. You've not kicked the habit, you're just feeding your habit with something different and hoping to hold the worst effects at bay.

The *replacement* strategy involves purposefully engaging your prefrontal cortex to modify the cognitive programme of your habit-craving limbic system. *Willpower comes from* using our rational, reasoning prefrontal cortex to picture the benefit of replacing a short-term habit with a long-term commitment. Remember, our prefrontal cortex isn't *always-on* like other brain areas: you must activate it with deep processing rather than superficial emotion-led thought. *Deep processing means creating a strong picture of a future benefit* that is as *real* in your mind as the temptation you will resist. It has to be powerful: the impulse control brake in your prefrontal cortex must be stronger than the *always-on* limbic system desire accelerator. This is what motivates long-term change and sustains self-discipline.

When I ask people what habit they most want to change, many say they want to kick eating crisps or biscuits in the evening, or consuming too many alcoholic drinks each night. Evening habits are particularly hard to kick because of another design flaw in our brains: our high energy consuming prefrontal cortex runs low on energy each day before the rest of our brain. Consequently, in the evening, our ever-active limbic system is busy pressing the accelerator pedal of our desire, but our rational prefrontal cortex is too tired to hit the brake hard enough. It is why willpower is lowest in the evening. It's no coincidence that people with healthy lifestyles and successful habits are often the people going to bed earlier. It's not just that they're tired from exercise, or can't wait to greet tomorrow, they know it's easier to simply sleep through that night-time window of temptation.

You may be thinking that good habits would be easier to form and bad habits easier to resist if we just used our prefrontal cortex more. Across many walks of life and many types of people, I have noticed that the most successful are those who are able to set aside their emotional reaction to

issues and really focus on using rational thinking to challenge automatic behaviours, beliefs and assumptions. They
have exactly the same brains as the rest of us; they are just
really good at purposefully engaging their prefrontal cortex
when it matters. This is something anyone can do. It is the
basis of the process of mastery.

Stages in Mastery

1. Find Your Strengths

Start by making a list of what you are good at. I'm not talking
about academic qualifications, though aptitude for certain
subjects should be listed. I am really talking about skills and
your qualities as a person. You may be great at putting ideas
into words, or be the most reliable or loyal person. You may
care about things more than most or be more imaginative
and dream bigger. You may also have what I called in **Cloud
2** a *pocket power*.

2. Challenge Your Beliefs

We are often held back by beliefs that we are completely unaware of. Develop awareness of why you hold certain beliefs
about issues like money, success, trust, family, risk, status,
authority and self-sufficiency. Re-visit past experiences and
think how these shaped your attitudes. Would you change
any? We have a choice about what meaning we assign to
beliefs, which we retain and which we discard. Knowing the
combination of your strengths and beliefs is *self-awareness*.

If you can add in acknowledgement of your flaws and weaknesses, acceptance of those you can't change and a desire to work on those you can, then you will be a rare person. Most people have no idea.

3. Develop Your Talents

Which abilities listed align with beliefs that are important to you? These are areas you should focus on to develop your talent. Becoming competent at something you believe is important is more fulfilling than becoming expert in something you believe is unimportant. List the talents you want to develop, break these into their constituent skill components and commit to how you will work on these. Think about how to employ an *improve mindset*.

4. Choose Your Path

This is the critical step in the mastery process: defining specific goals with a plan to achieve each one. Many people think they can't achieve mastery because it needs specialist knowledge. It doesn't. It just needs you to write down your ideas for what you will do to progress your goals. Ideas written down are a plan; ideas inside your head are dreams. The ideas can be exactly the same, but the outcome won't be. The very best plans make a daily habit or ritual of all the little things you want to progress, to keep things moving along.

5. Remove Distractions

Think about *where* you will work towards your goals; then remove all distractions from that place. Some distractions are always with us, like our phones and social media. If these eat up considerable time or focus, it's time to be radical. Turn it off. Think also about *how* you work. Some people confuse activity with effort; they argue that they're frantically busy but the endless flurry of activity is a strategy to avoid what really needs doing. Be honest – if it doesn't lie on the path towards your goals, why are you doing it?

One belief you may want to examine at this point is whether you believe willpower is a finite commodity. Since psychologists are unsure on this point, you can choose to believe what you want. If *you* choose to believe it is infinite, it will profoundly change your views on what you think is possible.

6. Learn to Love the Process

If you are a *Lyre Bird* rather than a *show pony* described in **Cloud 4** then you will find it easier to enjoy the process. If not, give it time. Some people enjoy the sense of possibility that the planning *Stages of Mastery* brings, whereas others need to start experiencing the accumulation of small successes first.

7. Discover Yourself

The self-awareness you gain through the early *Stages of Mastery* doesn't stop. Listen to your emotions, but don't let them get in the driving seat. You will continue to find out more about yourself and this may lead you to re-evaluate and refine some of your goals. This is good. It shows the process is working. It is foolish to cling to goals if your understanding of where to go has advanced.

8. Forgive Yourself

There will be times when you fail, or when progress is difficult; you may doubt your goals. Be kind, show self-compassion, which is explained in **Cloud 4**, and remember two things: everybody fails at some point, and you have already come a long way. The problem may be in the way you framed your goals; you don't have to be the *best* in your field, you just have to be *better* than you would otherwise be. Don't compare yourself to others; it never helps.

9. Draw Strength from Others

We reflect the characteristics of people we spend most time around; use this to your advantage by seeking out others with an *improve mindset* who are on their own path to *mastery*, even if their goals are very different to yours. It's sharing a process that matters, not common goals.

Conversely, if people in your life do not believe in you the way *you* believe in you, ask yourself what you gain from associating with them. Having someone useful to sharpen your axe on through animosity is OK; being held back isn't.

10. Pass It On

Mastery has no end point. Since we can always improve, it is an unattainable goal; but this doesn't make it less worthwhile. Devoting ourselves to something we can never complete is valuable for what it teaches us about humility and our place in the universe. The last stage of mastery is not about becoming perfect; it is passing on the benefit of what we learned to others. Later, we will look at how to *pay it forward* by passing on your knowledge.

Why Don't We listen?

People often find it odd when I talk about listening in the context of mastery. Surely listening is something we can all do without making any particular changes other than remembering to do a bit more of it?

As with many other simple-sounding things, the solution isn't easy. What we must master, which may take real effort, is the *not talking* bit of listening. This is related to impulse control and the deep-seated habits that determine our behaviours. People talk for many different reasons beyond sharing ideas; they talk because they are anxious, to validate themselves, to make other people like them or because they feel awkward when conversation pauses; some men are conditioned to believe they should take the conversational lead. Other people pathologically cannot listen. For them, what other people are saying is just the bit that happens whilst they are waiting to talk.

Most people don't *really* listen because they can't master their urge to talk. When I am working with clients, I use the expression SONAR as a reminder to *Sound Out Needs And Respond*. In other words; ask people questions, then shut up and really listen – focusing on what they *don't* say as well as what they *do* say – and then, and only then, do we talk to venture an opinion or solution.

As a basic strategy it works well, but like many skills it can be developed through mastery to become an extreme ability. I want to share the story of someone I knew who became a true SONAR master. I'm also going to stay with the analogy of SONAR which actually stands for *Sound Navigation and Ranging* and is, as you probably know, the underwater 'radar' used by submarines.

SONAR

In submarine movies like *The Hunt for Red October*, *Crimson Tide* and *Hunter Killer*, deadly undersea games of cat and mouse are punctuated by the 'ping-donk' of SONAR: the eyes and ears of submarines beneath the waves. Except real-life submarine warfare is nothing like that. It's far more interesting.

There are two types of SONAR on board submarines. *Active* SONAR is the one we know from films, with a distinctive 'ping' made by transducers emitting sound pulses into the water, and a 'donk' noise picked up by microphones listening for echoes from underwater objects. The strength and delay of these echoes produces the data telling the captain about the size, location, speed and bearing of an adversary, but only after a SONAR operator has sorted the signal from the irrelevant noise.

Nowadays, active SONAR is seldom used to hunt enemies. It can mislead and it can be evaded. Worse still, 'ping' signals you send tell others where you are. That's why modern submarines use a second system called *passive* SONAR, which isn't shown in the movies; partly because it doesn't produce filmic sound effects but also because we're not meant to know much about classified systems way above our pay grade. What we are cleared to know is that passive SONAR uses arrays of microphones embedded in submarine hulls to listen for other vessels. A skilled operator can interpret a passive SONAR trace to tell what shape a vessel is, how many engines it has, the number of propellers and even how many blades. In the right hands, this intelligence pinpoints exactly what you are dealing with. And they won't even know you're there.

So, what has this got to do with listening to people? The connection is that in business, as well as in submarines, winning is not always about how much firepower you have, it's often about how quiet you can be. When it comes to *really* listening, passive can be better than active.

This is the story of Jack and Jill, pretend names for two real people I enjoyed working with many years ago. Jill was bright, motivated and an excellent presenter, her down-to-earth manner made her popular with clients in the region where she'd grown up. One day, Jill and I were making a boardroom pitch to her largest client. Reflecting the scale of our proposal, Jill's client had brought along their head of every department: Legal, Operations, Compliance and Finance, to gain company-wide buy-in. I introduced the meeting, and Jill started her presentation. After 20 minutes and some questions, the managing director said, '*Thank you Jill, I think we've heard enough. I'd like a show of hands from my Board to see if we can move straight to Terms of Engagement.*'

I'll never forget Jill's response; '*You can't, I've not finished my presentation.*' Jill hadn't noticed that she'd reached her objective; she was still set on transmit. It was her default setting. She had her receivers blocked.

Jack was Jill's boss. His default setting was receive. Jack was the least likely person you'd expect as sales head of a fiercely competitive firm; he was quiet, unassuming and extraordinarily intense. If you met Jack, you'd take him for a lawyer, or perhaps Chief Intensity Officer of the Intense Corporation.

When he visited clients Jack made a point of arriving early, to sit in reception and listen. He might grab a coffee in the client's canteen. When he spoke, he never pitched products or sales ideas. He would stay quiet for most of a meeting, and when he finally spoke it would be to offer an observation: '*I see your call centre is very busy*' or '*It looks like you've expanded your marketing team*' even '*there are lots of new registrations in your car park.*' Where he would go next was awe-inspiring: sharing insights on how to manage call centre workloads, on ways to train new marketers, on ideas to boost retention if staff were earning big bonuses and may be tempted away. I never saw a client who wasn't staggered by Jack's insight into their business. Jack spent his time listening, finding high potential firms who had hit growth barriers that they may not see, but which he could help ease. Jill asked the right questions, but her *transmit* could drown out her *receive*. Jack didn't even transmit let alone deploy his firepower until he'd finished listening.

That's the point of this story. Your active SONAR systems are useful; broadcasting questions and awaiting responses, but these have limitations. In some situations you betray too much; outgoing communication may over-ride incoming data. You may miss subtle cues or valuable data. When you learn to engage your passive SONAR system, the really valuable information is gained. Jack picked up a myriad of tiny signals across all frequencies and used it to build a far more insightful picture of customers. He dived deep into their needs. He conquered his need to always transmit. He achieved mastery over his need to talk in order that he could *really* listen.

Passing It On

As we progress through our working life our motivation changes. At the conclusion of our careers or when we reach our desired niche, financial or business success may be less important. We may instead think in terms of personal fulfilment and passing a legacy to others.

Coaching and mentoring provide an opportunity to pass on experience and gain satisfaction by contributing to the development of a new generation of leaders. Research proves that mentoring benefits are reciprocal and mentors report increased job and career fulfilment. Management textbooks typically treat coaching, mentoring and feedback as very different:

Feedback is backward looking and designed to identify specific task-based actions or wider behaviours that need to be improved.

Coaching is forward looking and uses practice, repetition and visualisation to achieve specified performance gains so someone reaches their potential.

Mentoring is the sharing of knowledge and experience to help someone define goals, develop strategies, find motivation and achieve personal growth.

All three methods share an aim of helping people improve future outcomes. There are key differences: because coaching is forward looking and feedback isn't, coaching focuses on behaviours that are not yet exhibited. Coaching may, like mentoring, touch on motivation; but is unlikely to be as directive or involve much self-disclosure. My own view is that there are no hard-and-fast boundaries, how you approach performance conversations depends partly upon the person, but mainly on the team culture you've developed. There is no reason why feedback can't touch upon aspects of coaching by looking at future behaviours, or why coaching shouldn't look at motivation strategies or even individual life-goals.

The world of sports performance coaching includes many of the aspects listed and offers valuable insights for business leaders. Forgetting definitions and adopting the *mindset of a coach* gives you a wider range of techniques to manage individual behaviour and build effective teams.

The Art of Feedback

As rock fans know, feedback is the noise created when guitar strings pick up secondary vibrations from speakers. Used well, feedback provides striking reinforcement; when utilised badly it's unlistenable. It's the same dilemma you face with your team: how do you ensure feedback always hits the right note?

Many managers are loath to use feedback because they don't enjoy it. They find it confrontational, they feel awkward addressing behaviours with a personal basis and they worry their authority may be challenged. They agonise over whether to let something slide whilst knowing full well it won't fix itself.

Other managers just thrive on finding faults in others and believe it is their role to constantly point these out. This is the sad paradox of feedback; the managers most likely to dish out loads of feedback tend to be the ones who use it badly. Thankfully, few leaders are like this. Most of us feel a bit hesitant tackling performance issues. If this sounds like you, take comfort that caution is a good thing, your reticence arises from your empathy and insight. These qualities pretty much guarantee you are thoughtful, well-intentioned and capable of being highly effective at providing feedback. Giving effective feedback is a skill you can develop; you simply need to learn how to identify issues quickly and build your confidence in delivery. In short, you need a framework that helps you know how to proceed.

There is an awful lot of advice in management books about giving feedback. I find most of what is written either too simplistic, or so academic that it ignores the practicalities and complexity of trying to help real people in real-world workplaces. Here are my own top 10 feedback rules.

1. Feedback Is Always Private

Performance feedback is always private, however tempting it may be to give someone a public roasting; that says you want to vent, not fix performance. Feedback should be given behind closed doors, in a calm setting that allows both people to fully focus. Respecting someone's privacy doesn't just mean conducting one-on-one meetings. It means allowing people the dignity of a meeting without colleagues knowing what is going on. Don't immediately haul someone into your office. Summon them later when you'll both benefit from clear heads and more insight.

2. Feedback Doesn't Punish, It Improves

It's natural to feel disappointed or angry when someone's actions fall below a required standard, but feedback isn't their punishment. It's designed to help them improve. Shouting, frowning or using hostile body language don't help. Feedback must be well-intentioned and based on a belief that a person is capable of changing their behaviour or deserves a chance to prove they can. Without you pulling any punches on the impact of their behaviour, people must hear you say you expect them to change and fully believe they can. If behaviour caused harms that require sanctions then that crosses the boundary from feedback into a disciplinary process, which is a different thing entirely.

3. Feedback Must Focus on Behaviour

Some things you can't change, like someone's level of intelligence, so this is off-limits to feedback. Focus only on behaviour you can change over time like role-specific performance; if feedback won't fix this, then designing a training and development plan or finding an appropriate-level role are the solutions. Feedback can only remedy specific instances of behaviour. It may be true that someone's overall ability isn't good enough for their role, but unless you can find specific behaviours they can modify, then feedback is not your solution.

4. Feedback Should Be Timely

The best time for feedback is whilst events are still fresh in the memory, but after a brief opportunity to reflect so someone is ready to hear what you say. This may sound obvious, but you will be surprised how much feedback is given too early: in the heat of the moment without enough thought, or after procrastinating, by which point recall will have faded. In most situations, the time to give feedback is later the same day, or for more serious issues in a meeting arranged for the following day. It's hard to convince someone an issue is urgent or important if you've let time go by.

5. Feedback Is a Process

It's unlikely you'll have one intervention that instantly solves all someone's performance issues. You're more likely to have a series of interactions, so be patient and play a strategic game. Confronting somebody with a list of a dozen issues will not help. Keep the list to yourself and address two or three at a time in order of urgency or importance. Arrange a follow-up review that gives you an opportunity to recognise progress and introduce the next issues on your list. There is a flipside to dedicating time to a feedback process for improving individual performance and team effectiveness, that is, when considerable time is consumed by one person who is stubbornly not responding to input. Unless the person is irreplaceable in a key role, you must consider how your time could benefit the wider team, and let that person go. For now, you will have a hole in your team. But at least you won't have an asshole.

6. Feedback Must Be Specific

Humans are prone to generalisation, mainly because our brain is wired to see patterns. If we witness a single action, we may automatically register it as another example of a trait, for example, interrupting colleagues or being late. Even when this is the latest in a series of similar behaviours, don't be tempted to say someone is 'always' interrupting or 'never' on time. People react to generalisations by challenging the degree to which it is fair or accurate. Feedback should relate to a specific example, they were late to yesterday's meeting and talked across two other colleagues. If you give them a specific instance, they cannot deny their behaviour. Lastly, use the past tense to describe behaviour: using the present tense could indicate that you are making a general assumption not a specific observation.

7. Feedback Is About Impacts

Hopefully, you are unlikely to get a toddler-like 'Why should I?' in response to feedback but the thought may still be running through someone's mind. Well-designed feedback heads that off by making someone aware of the effect their behaviour has and why that is unacceptable for example, if individuals couldn't contribute in a meeting because they were talked over or if a group had to cut their agenda because a meeting started late. In complex businesses, front-line staff may be unaware of down-stream impacts of making exceptions or not following procedures. Never assume people understand the impact of their behaviour on business processes as well as you; they don't have your experience or business knowledge so take this opportunity to share your insight.

8. Feedback Must Acknowledge Intention

Sometimes people do the wrong thing or bend rules because they think it is appropriate or helpful. For example, sharing information with a customer that they shouldn't, or making exceptions to procedures without seeing the impact. Feedback discussions must always explore intention; you cannot assume you know why someone acted as they did. When you acknowledge a good intention behind someone's actions, this doesn't undermine your feedback. In fact, showing that you understand and do not blame their motivation will make someone more likely to want to understand why new behaviour is required. Conversely, if an intention behind someone's behaviour was negative for example, laziness, malice or taking undue credit, then this attitude will need addressing alongside the behaviour you want to change.

9. Feedback Can Be a Dialogue

When you have invested time building team rapport, performance conversations will not necessarily be one-sided instructions of 'I need you to do this' For people handling challenging tasks and complex decisions, it is appropriate to ask: '*How do you think you could have done it differently?*,' '*What alternatives were available?*' or '*Which outcomes may have changed?*' By providing answers for themselves, a two-way discussion incentivises team members to learn and change. This works the other way; you may learn of problems you are unaware of. People may be working around issues that you could solve with a better operational process. What you saw as an individual performance issue could be a valuable early warning.

10. Beyond Feedback: Coaching, Appraisal and Mentoring

A culture where feedback is seen as commonplace and constructive is an excellent platform for a regular self-appraisal process where individuals discuss performance with their line manager. By comparing their own ratings of their performance with the views of their manager they can mutually agree development goals and the means by which those goals will be supported. You will find that you no longer have to 'hover' to find the right moment to give feedback: your team will come to you and ask for it. You have earned the right to be their performance coach.

Then one day, someone will come to you and place their future in your hands: they will ask for career advice. Not asking whether they should seek promotion or sign up for some training, but *'where on earth should I go next?'* Counselling someone on this is a big responsibility. If you accept it – and you should – you must accept a possible outcome is that this person must leave your team to get to where they need to be. It is *never* the right answer to persuade them to stay because you need them. By all means, tell them they are valued and you want them to stay; but the conversation is about what *they* need and want. I use a story I call *rockpools*.

Rockpools

My childhood holiday memories aren't of sunny and sandy foreign resorts. I remember rocky, rainy British beaches. I wouldn't change a thing, because I had rockpools. I loved the thrill of peering into the depths of a rockpool, pulling aside seaweed fronds and gently turning rocks to expose the breathtaking richness of intertidal life. A rockpool may look like a tranquil haven, but it's not. The occupants are either looking for lunch, trying not to become lunch or both. It's a harsh habitat: rockpool life must cope with swings in temperature and oxygen levels and the ever-present risk of drying out.

As a child, I wondered whether it was better to be a creature that stayed in a familiar little pool or one that could swim to a bigger, wilder place. Then I grew up, got a series of jobs and realised I was right back in the rockpools. *Have I outgrown where I am? Is this environment getting better or worse? Are familiar risks easier than new challenges? Would I thrive better in a bigger pool?*

It's hard to see the exact point at which we outgrow our rockpool. Rockpool creatures are highly sensitive to their surroundings. Like them we must pay attention to what's around us. If you don't believe in your current company like you once did, if the effort you put in is no longer appreciated, if your work doesn't match your interests or stretch your skills and there's no way to change this then your rockpool is drying out. You can stay, using a thick shell to withstand the stress like a barnacle or a limpet, or you can swim away.

Sometimes staying is appropriate. Businesses go through cycles and economic, commercial, managerial and strategic changes are like the tide: ebbing and flowing, always temporary. Company reshuffles settle, staffing and resource issues may be resolved. The tide will either eventually flow your way, or it won't, and you will leave.

The other possibility is that the discomfort you feel isn't about what your company is going through and everything to do with you: you've outgrown your rockpool. If your own thinking, capability and ambition have evolved and you have no opportunity to use these then the next high tide marks your escape opportunity. Leaving your rockpool to find a bigger pool or swim freely in the ocean is not without risk. As with tides, timing is everything. If you work in a sector that is sensitive to business cycles or driven by swings in demand, then it's easier to swim away on a flow tide when the water is rising, when the business is doing well. However, it is human nature to start thinking about leaving when a business is doing badly: on an ebb tide when falling water levels across the whole sector can seriously limit choices.

This creates a paradox that can ensnare people. *We often want to leave precisely when it might be a bad opportunity, and stay when it could be a better opportunity to leave.* To avoid the trap, use these rockpool escape plan pointers to remove emotion from decisions:

Are you learning? This doesn't have to be formal study or even specific technical or professional knowledge. But it is vital to keep learning things that you can use in future to carry you to success.

Do you feel valued? If your input, contribution and opinion aren't valued, you'll never feel fulfilled even when other supposed measures of value like salary or job title are fine.

Are you still engaged? We're all engaged differently: for some of us having fun is key, for others it is regular new challenges or successful relationships with colleagues and customers. You'll know if you disengage: you clock watch and find excuses to avoid the extra mile.

Is your stress OK? Nobody loves their job 100 per cent of every day. But if you feel permanently over-worked and under-valued be aware of signs of physical and mental stress and monitor these in relation to your job. If in doubt, get out.

Can you swim forwards? If you've been in the same role for three to five years and you can't see opportunities or ways forward; if the only thing in front of you is a rock, then it's time to swim sideways or out of your pool.

If someone answers all five questions and scores *below four*, it's time to plan the next move. Your advice might be to update their CV and draw up a checklist of what a new role must offer, including the chance to develop their interests, passions, skills and specific abilities. I'm often struck by the degree to which successful people have aligned their career with their personal interests. It's not a coincidence; everyone deserves to work in an area that ignites their enthusiasm and passion. But people must decide what this looks like *before* they set out. We are only ready to leave our rockpool when we can swim in positive currents pulling us *towards what we do want*. If we follow negative currents pushing us away from what we don't want, we'll be a jellyfish with no control over where we end up.

The wonderful thing about rockpools is that some creatures make them a permanent home and others are just passing through. Most amazing of all, every tiny rockpool becomes periodically connected to other rockpools, the entire sea and the vast mighty ocean. If people get their timing right, and are clear about what they want, there are no limits.

There is no more rewarding feeling than knowing that you are contributing towards someone's future success: building the next generation of leaders, helping people identify their goals and find strategies to move towards them. Not only are these the right thing to do but research shows that passing on the benefit of experience and knowledge through processes like coaching and mentoring contributes greatly to the satisfaction of people in the coaching role. Just like respect, it is reciprocal; as you give, you get back. That's how great people make other people feel great.

And this is the closest thing this book has to a conclusion. That life should be lived not just for material benefits, but as a continuous process of learning and growth, driven by our curiosity to become better at something for its own rewards and in order to find opportunities to help others.

Through the act of striving to become better at something, we allow ourselves to become changed by the process; we become better at being the person we truly are and the version of ourselves we want to be.

> *Every person has their own path to perfection, and we are re-born in order to carry out the tasks necessary to work out our fate.*[2]
>
> The Nine Cloud Dream, Kim Man-Jung

Acknowledgements

Stuart would like to thank Sebastian who inspires him by refusing to believe anything is impossible until he has tried it, and Isabelle who has patiently shared her encouragement and deep knowledge of psychology. He would like to thank Milli for generously allowing him the opportunity and space to write a book, and Adrian for providing shovelfuls of grit to help create the ideas in it.

Adrian is indebted to Rosie and Harry for continuing to challenge his thinking, and to Louise for all her honesty and wise counsel. He would also like to thank James Poole for his rock-solid support and state his gratitude to Annie Knight and all the team at Wiley.

Appendix

1. *International Journal of Behavioral Science. 2011; 6(1):73-92*
2. Adapted. The English translation made by Heinz Insu Fenkl, Professor of English at The State University of New York, New Paltz reads: 'Each man has his own path to perfection, and each is reborn in order to carry out the things necessary to work out his Karma.' This original text includes Kim Man-Jung's reference to the Buddhist religious principle that, through reincarnation, adherents strive to rid themselves of karma acquired in previous existences. If you get a chance to read Fenkl's translation of Kim Man-Jung's The Nine Cloud Dream you should. It is a beautiful story

Index